The Sous Vide Recipe Book

Norma Miller

A HOW TO BOOK

ROBINSON

ROBINSON

First published in Great Britain in 2015 by Robinson

A CIP catalogue record for this book
is available from the British Library.

ISBN: 978-0-7160-2334-0

Typeset in the UK by Basement Press, Glaisdale
Printed and bound in Great Britain by Clays Ltd, St Ives plc

Papers used by Robinson are from well-managed forests
and other responsible sources

MIX
Paper from
responsible sources
FSC
www.fsc.org
FSC® C104740

Robinson
An imprint of
Little, Brown Book Group
Carmelite House
50 Victoria Embankment
London EC4Y 0DY

An Hachette UK Company
www.hachette.co.uk

www.littlebrown.co.uk

How To Books are published by Robinson, an imprint of Little, Brown Book Group.
We welcome proposals from authors who have first-hand experience of their subjects.
Please set out the aims of your book, its target market and its suggested
contents in an email to Nikki.Read@howtobooks.co.uk

Contents

Introduction

Sous vide machines are among the most striking innovations to make their way from the chefs' kitchens into our homes. As a result, the domestic cooking experience could well be completely transformed.

Fundamental to the success of the sous vide method, which cooks food in vacuum-sealed pouches in a hot water bath, is its ability to control cooking temperatures. Fillet steaks, salmon, chicken breast, venison, in fact meat and fish of all kinds, and fruit and vegetables too, all need to be cooked at an optimum temperature – not too high, not too low – in order to produce outstanding results. Sous vide is simply better than any other cooking process at achieving this. It does it every time with consistency and precision. The food that emerges from the water bath in the sealed pouches will be tender, succulent and full of flavour.

Another distinctive feature of sous vide cooking is the way it can be adapted to modern busy lifestyles. Cooking in the sous vide machine can often take longer than conventional methods. This is especially true of meat and vegetables, which can take several hours or even days. On the plus side is the fact that the sous vide machine, once started, can be left unattended throughout the cooking time.

The sous vide cooking process naturally breaks down into three stages. Stage 1 is the preparation of the food to go into the pouches, which are then vacuum-sealed. In stage 2, the machine is set to the required temperature for the recipe. When at temperature, the sealed pouches are lowered into the water bath and the timer set for the cooking time. Stage 3 sees the finishing of the dish. Sauces and accompaniments can be prepared at this stage, and meat or fish can be seared.

The three stages don't need to be performed in quick succession. They can be separated by hours or even a few days. Both before and after the water-bath stage, the sealed pouches can be ice-chilled and then placed in the fridge or freezer until needed. Guidance on how to do this safely, so as to preserve the quality of the food, can be found later in the book (see page 7). This all enables busy people – as most of us are these days – to plan ahead, and means you never need to spend too long in the kitchen.

Sous vide cooking can also be great fun. You learn to think about food in very different ways, and the techniques involved are easy to acquire and really rather ingenious. Plus you can always do a bit of experimenting and you can get great results.

What Is Cooking Sous Vide?

The essence of sous vide is the application of science and technology to food. The technology, which has been available to chefs for some time, has now led to the manufacture of sous vide machines for the home cook in tandem with vacuum-sealing machines for the bags to be used as food pouches in the water bath.

Science relates to the way the food in the vacuum-sealed pouch cooks evenly and retains all its juices during the cooking process. Science also determines how immersion of the filled pouches in a controlled water bath allows heat to reach the food more efficiently than is the case with the air that surrounds food on the hob or in an oven. Cooking at lower temperatures becomes possible with sous vide, and as this is beneficial, the flavour of food is frequently enhanced.

Equipment

To cook sous vide recipes at home, you'll need, a domestic sous vide (water bath) machine, food-grade plastic bags suitable for cooking in a sous vide machine, and a vacuum-sealing machine.

The sous vide machine looks rather like a free-standing metal box with a control panel display on the outside and a separate power lead. The other removable parts are a lid, a grill and a rack. The insulated lid doubles up as a tray when turned over. When you lift the cooked food pouches out of the water bath, you can put them on the tray to catch any drips.

The grill sits in the base of the water bath and allows the hot water to move under the food pouches.

The rack can be used to hold individual food pouches vertically in the water bath to give even cooking. The food must be kept below the surface of the water during cooking, so the rack can also be used horizontally to keep floating pouches submerged in the water.

Food-grade plastic bags of varying sizes must be of the right type, specifically made for cooking in the sous vide machine.

Before cooking, the filled food pouches need to be sealed, so use a vacuum-sealing machine to suck the air out of the pouch and heat-seal the open end to give an airtight pouch.

Other useful, but not essential, pieces of equipment are a fridge thermometer to check the temperature of the appliance is correct, and a culinary blow torch to sear cooked meat, fish or desserts.

Care and Cleaning

- Read the Important Safety Advice section below.
- Always unplug the machine before emptying and cleaning.
- Wait until the water has cooled before removing the racks and pouring the water away.
- To clean, simply wipe the inside and outside of the machine with a soft, dry cloth.
- If a food pouch has leaked or burst, then clean the inside of the cold, empty machine with soapy water, rinse and dry.
- Do not clean the machine in a dishwasher or immerse in water.

Important Safety Advice

Much of this advice should be common sense when using any kitchen appliance but it's always useful to remind ourselves of kitchen safety rules.

- Machines vary, so read the manufacturer's instruction manual.
- The sous vide machine must be positioned on a stable, heatproof surface and not near the edge of a work surface.
- Keep the surrounding areas clear and free from clutter.
- Ensure there is adequate space around the machine for air to circulate.
- Only use the machine indoors.
- Make sure the power cord doesn't run underneath the machine, doesn't touch hot surfaces and doesn't get wet.
- Take care as, when in use, the surfaces of the machine, as well as the water, will become very hot.
- Do not move the machine while in use as it will be hot.
- Use oven gloves and tongs when removing the pouches from the hot water bath.
- Make sure the water is above the FILL level mark but below the MAX level mark.
- Wait until the water has cooled before emptying it out.
- Do not put the machine away until it is cold.
- Keep children and pets away from the machine when in use.
- If any faults occur with your sous vide machine, always contact the manufacturer.

The Basics

This section gives you step-by-step information on using your sous vide machine. Since appliances vary, do read this in conjunction with your manufacturer's information.

Preparing Food to Cook Sous Vide

Follow these general guidelines and prepare the food as indicated in the recipes.

Beef, lamb and pork can be cooked successfully in a variety of ways, either on or off the bone. Wrap any sharp bones in parchment paper.

Poultry and game are best cooked as portions, as air inside the body cavity of whole birds may cause the food pouch to float, resulting in uneven cooking. Wrap any sharp bones in parchment paper. The skin doesn't sear or brown as it would in an oven so I remove the skin before cooking.

Fish and shellfish cooked at low temperatures hold on to all their flavour. They have a lovely texture and won't overcook, provided you don't exceed the recommended cooking time. Once you've tried this, you won't want to cook fish any other way.

Fresh green vegetables can lose a little colour when cooked in a water bath. However, it's very easy to keep them a brighter green by blanching them before use. Drop the vegetables into boiling water for 10 seconds, then immediately drain and put them into a bowl of ice-cold water until cold, then drain.

Root vegetables, such as carrots and beetroots, and other vegetables, such as peppers, hold their vivid colours and cook through evenly without the outside becoming overcooked. They are cooked at a higher temperature than meat.

Other vegetables, such as swedes, turnips and aubergines, can be rather bitter or pungent in taste when cooked sous vide, so I tend not to use them.

Fruits also retain their lovely flavours and colour. Fruits that would usually start to brown when cooked – such as apples and pears – have a much better colour when cooked sous vide.

Eggs must be cooked until pasteurised. Whole eggs are cooked without vacuum-sealing.

Spices need to be used sparingly as the cooking process intensifies the flavours, although they can still be added to the pouch before cooking. Use fresh **herbs** or powdered rubs or flavourings, such as herbed butters and flavoured oils. Don't **salt** meat until after cooking.

4

Alcohol – wine or spirits – needs to be used with care. First heat the wine or spirits in a pan on the hob to drive off the alcohol before adding it to the food pouch. This will preserve the flavour of the wine or spirits, otherwise they can give a metallic taste to food cooked sous vide.

Filling and Sealing the Food Pouches

As well as the type of food to be cooked, the cooking time provided also relates to the thickness of the food in the pouch. The food will also cook more efficiently if the pouches are not too full, so don't overfill the bags and aim to have the food in an even, single layer, if possible. The recipes here use between one and four bags.

If some of the food items you are going to vacuum-pack are liquid, then I often find it easier to freeze liquids – such as stock, tomatoes or juices – before adding them to the pouches so that they are easier to handle.

To fill a bag, first turn back the opening to keep it clean – any bits of food sticking to the surface will prevent the bag from sealing securely, resulting in leakage. Put soft foods in the bag with heavier items on top, then pour in any liquids that will drop to the bottom. If there are flavourings – such as lemon zest, herbs or spices – shake the bag gently to mix the ingredients together. Turn back the clean edge so the food pouch is ready for sealing.

Use the vacuum-sealer to suck the air out of the filled food pouch and heat-seal the open end to ensure it is airtight. If there are soft ingredients or liquids in the pouch, they may start to be drawn up to the end of the pouch and into the machine, so make sure you stop the vacuum process quickly. Just press out as much air as possible with your hand and seal the pouch. Slightly massage the pouch when sealed to spread the ingredients to a single layer.

Using the Sous Vide Machine

Always fill the machine with water before switching on. Initially pour enough water into the machine to cover the bottom rack and to reach the FILL level mark.

Put on the lid, turn on the machine and the water-temperature indicator will illuminate and show the current water temperature – the digital indicator can be altered to show either Celsius or Fahrenheit readings. It is then easy to set the water temperature required for the recipe. The default cooking temperature setting for the machine I use is 60°C/140°F, and your machine will use this or a similar temperature. This is the setting I've used in many of the recipes. To set a different temperature for a recipe, use the increase and decrease arrows.

Once you have selected your temperature, press the start button and a red light shows that the water is heating. When it has reached the required temperature, the light turns green and the food pouches can then be placed in the machine.

Use the pouch rack to hold individual food pouches vertically in the water bath – this keeps them sufficiently spaced to give even cooking. Don't put very large food pouches horizontally in the water bath so that they cover the entire base and touch the sides, as this will stop the movement of water. When the pouches are added, the water level will rise. The food in the pouches must be below the surface of the water during cooking. If necessary, use a rack horizontally to keep any floating pouches fully submerged. If the water goes above the MAX level mark once the pouches are in position, carefully remove the excess hot water using a jug.

Close the machine again, and wait for the water bath to return to the correct temperature. Now set the cooking timer to the required time and leave until the process is complete.

Recipe Timing

The length of the cooking time depends on the thickness of the food rather than the weight. For example, if you double the thickness of a steak it could take up to four times as long to cook. This is because of the time it takes for the centre of the meat to be cooked, and why it is important to pack the pouches carefully, as explained above.

Foods can be cooked at their desired serving temperature and kept for quite long periods of time in the sous vide machine without any loss of flavour, or they can be cooked at a higher temperature for a shorter period of time.

Times will vary considerably. Tough cuts of meat need longer cooking times, often 6–8 hours to tenderize the meat. Tough, fatty cuts of meat, such as leg of lamb or spare ribs, can cook for up to three days. The result is delicious, tender meat that will fall apart when you serve it. Tender meats such as lamb chop, rack of lamb and sirloin steaks are cooked to serving temperature for up to 4 hours.

The times for cooking in the water bath in each recipe give a maximum and a minimum. Cook for the minimum time and the food will be cooked through to the serving temperature. It can then be served straight away, or it can be held in the water bath at that temperature up to the maximum time given. The food can be served and eaten at any time between the minimum and maximum timings and the food will not alter. Just practise the timings with your favourite ingredients.

Do not cook the pouches below the temperature indicated in the recipes or for less than the minimum length of time given in each recipe.

After Cooking in the Sous Vide Machine

You won't get a crisp, crunchy or crusty finish to food by cooking sous vide. Instead it will look as though it has been steamed or poached, which is fine for white meats, fish and shellfish as they only need the addition of a sauce to complete the dish. If you prefer, searing meat or fish very quickly on all sides in a hot, oiled frying pan, or brushing with oil and putting under a hot grill, will give that familiar browned finish. Or use a culinary blow torch, although this brings another set of safety issues into play. Searing has to be done quickly as the food will continue cooking.

Using the Fridge and Freezer

Having cooked the food, however, you may want to store the pouches in the fridge or freezer. They are convenient to store, and if you have chilled or frozen food pouches of vegetables, meat or fish readily available in your fridge or freezer, you have a really convenient way of creating a complete meal at a moment's notice. You can therefore ice-chill and refrigerate or freeze the prepared pouches between stages.

Remember that if you are not going to cook them immediately, it's important not to leave raw or cooked vacuum-sealed food pouches lying around on the kitchen surfaces. Chill them thoroughly as soon as possible by submerging the pouches in a bowl of iced water, made with equal quantities of ice and water. As the ice melts, keep topping up with more ice and turning the pouches occasionally until the food is completely cold. Then the pouches can be dried and put in the fridge or freezer. The recipes indicate the storage times that will give you optimum flavour and texture.

To reheat a chilled or frozen food pouch, put it into the water bath at the same temperature it was cooked at for about 45 minutes until heated through.

About the Recipes

I've cooked these recipes using a small sous vide machine of the type that has been designed for domestic use in your own kitchen.

- In the recipes I refer to a 'water bath' – this is a domestic sous vide machine.
- All the preparation and cooking processes for each recipe are straightforward and easy to follow.
- For convenience, the recipe ingredients are listed in the order in which they are used. Though they are given in imperial as well as metric, you will find the metric measurements easier.
- All spoon measures are level unless otherwise stated.

- The recipes are often adaptable, and you can easily substitute interchangeable ingredients, such as nectarines for peaches or fennel leaves for sprigs of dill.
- For these recipes I have used a mixture of fresh seasonal produce, store-cupboard ingredients, canned foods, as well as some frozen items. I also keep a wide selection of small jars of pastes, rubs, dried herbs and spices. They are a quick and easy way to add instant flavour to the meat, fish, vegetables or fruits in the food pouches. I grow herbs in pots so I have a fresh supply almost all the year round.
- You have bought the equipment and will be spending time making these recipes, so do use good-quality ingredients to get the best results.
- If you are preparing food for someone who has a food allergy, be sure to study the list of ingredients carefully.
- Most of the recipes make two to four servings, depending on whether they are eaten as a snack, a starter or a main course.
- Throughout the book, there are plenty of serving suggestions and hints and tips to go with the recipes.
- Keep a good supply of ice cubes in your freezer for rapidly chilling the food pouches.

Adapting Your Favourite Recipes for the Sous Vide Machine

You probably have several favourite recipes that you'd usually cook on the hob, in the oven or in a slow cooker. Many of these may be suitable to adapt to cooking with a sous vide machine – you just need to experiment a little. Look at your favourite recipe and break it down into sections. For example, decide which parts can be cooked sous vide. The main protein part (meat or fish) with a spice rub or fresh herbs can go in the sous vide machine. Is there a sauce to pour over the vegetables? This can be made as the food pouches are cooking in the water bath. Meat or fish cooked sous vide can always be quickly seared in a hot pan, under a hot grill or with a culinary blow torch to brown.

1
Vegetables

Sous vide cooking works really well with almost all our most familiar vegetables. Be prepared for the results to exceed your expectations! Look out for your personal favourites or regular standbys in this recipe selection, or try something different. You'll find it couldn't be easier. Thinly slice vegetables or cut them into bite-sized pieces, add a little seasoning, arrange in a food pouch, vacuum pack and put into the water bath alongside a pouch of meat or fish. It's a neat way to produce a whole meal.

When cooking vegetables sous vide remember to:
• Wash all vegetables thoroughly before using.
• Before using in your selected recipe, blanch green vegetables in boiling water for 10 seconds, then immediately drain and put them into a bowl of ice-cold water until cold. This will help to preserve the colour.
• The texture of vegetables can soften if they are in the water bath longer than their cooking time, but this is perfect when making soups or purées.
• If using frozen vegetables, add 5–10 minutes to the cooking time.

Leek and Potato Soup

A substantial, filling dish, this versatile soup is always a favourite. You can serve it hot or chill it, swirl in a spoonful of soured cream and serve it cold.

Serves: 2–4
Water bath cooking time: 1–2 hours

1 leek
1 medium potato
1 small onion
1 tbsp olive oil
2 tbsp vegetable stock
Pinch of ground thyme
Salt and freshly ground white pepper
To finish the dish
150ml/¼ pint vegetable or chicken stock
1 tbsp chopped parsley
2 tbsp crème fraîche
Olive oil or chilli oil (optional)
Hot crusty bread, to serve

1   Fill the water bath and preheat to 84°C/183°F.
2   Finely chop the leek, potato and onion.
3   Put the prepared vegetables into a large food pouch and add the olive oil, stock, thyme and a little seasoning. Shake the pouch to mix the ingredients. Push the ingredients into a single, even layer and vacuum-seal.
4   When at temperature, put the pouch into the water bath. Put the rack horizontally on top of the pouch to keep it submerged. Cover with the lid and cook for 1–2 hours.
5   To finish the dish, pour the stock into a pan and bring to the boil. Lift the pouch from the water bath and pour the contents into the pan of stock. Use a stick blender to whizz the soup to the consistency you prefer – chunky or smooth. Stir in the parsley and season to taste.
6   Swirl a spoonful of crème fraîche on the top and drizzle over a few drops of olive oil or chilli oil, if using. Serve immediately with hot crusty bread. Alternatively, you can cool and chill the soup, then serve it with a swirl of soured cream.

At the end of step 4, the vacuum-sealed food pouch can be ice-chilled and refrigerated for up to four days, or frozen.

Celeriac and Carrots

As its flavour is a mixture of celery and parsley, celeriac makes a lovely pairing with carrots.

Serves: 2–4
Water bath cooking time: 45 minutes–2 hours

½ celeriac, weighing about 350g/12oz
4 carrots
2 tbsp unsalted butter
1 tsp clear honey
1 tsp lemon juice
Salt and freshly milled black pepper

1 Fill the water bath and preheat to 84°C/183°F.
2 Peel the vegetables and cut into bite-sized chunks.
3 Put the prepared vegetables into a large food pouch. Add the butter, honey, lemon juice and a little salt and pepper. Push the ingredients into a single, even layer and vacuum-seal.
4 When at temperature, put the pouch into the water bath. Put the rack horizontally on top of the pouch to keep it submerged. Cover with the lid and cook for 45 minutes–2 hours.
5 Lift the pouch from the water bath. Remove the vegetables and serve immediately.

At the end of step 4, the vacuum-sealed food pouch can be ice-chilled and refrigerated for up to four days, or frozen.

Carrots, Parsnips and Peas with a Cheese Crust

If you are using frozen peas, add an extra 5–10 minutes to the cooking time.

Serves: 2–4
Water bath cooking time: 40 minutes–1¼ hours

2 carrots
2 parsnips
280g/10oz podded peas, fresh or frozen
3 tbsp unsalted butter
2 tbsp vegetable stock
Salt and freshly milled black pepper
To finish the dish
1 tbsp vegetable oil
4 tbsp fresh breadcrumbs
2 tbsp grated mature Cheddar or Red Leicester cheese
2 tbsp freshly chopped parsley

1   Fill the water bath and preheat to 84°C/183°F.
2   Trim the carrots and parsnips, peel and cut into bite-sized pieces.
3   Put the carrots, parsnips and peas into three separate food pouches. Divide the butter, stock and a little seasoning among the pouches. Push the ingredients into a single, even layer and vacuum-seal.
4   When at temperature, put the pouches of vegetables into the pouch holder and lower into the water bath. If using frozen peas, add them at the same time; if using fresh, add them 10 minutes later. Put the rack horizontally on top of the pouches to keep them submerged. Cover with the lid and cook for 40 minutes–1¼ hours.
5   Heat the oil in a frying pan and, when hot, add the breadcrumbs. Cook for a few minutes, stirring all the time, until the crumbs are lightly browned. Remove the pan from the heat and quickly stir in the grated cheese and chopped parsley, then season with salt and pepper to taste.
6   Preheat the grill to high.
7   Lift the pouches from the water bath. Remove all the vegetables and put them into a wide, heated, flameproof dish. Thinly scatter the crumb mixture over the top and grill for a few minutes until the cheese has melted. Alternatively, you can use a culinary blow torch to do this. Serve immediately.

At the end of step 4, the vacuum-sealed food pouches can be refrigerated for up to four days.

Charred Fennel

Cooked fennel has the light, delicate flavour of star anise. A ridged frying pan will give attractive charred lines to the fennel.

Serves: 2–4
Water bath cooking time: 1–2 hours

1 tbsp lemon juice
2 small fennel bulbs
2 tsp olive oil
Salt and freshly milled black pepper
To finish the dish
Oil and butter, for frying

1   Fill the water bath and preheat to 84°C/183°F.
2   Pour the lemon juice into a small, shallow bowl of water. Trim the fennel bulbs and cut into 1cm/½in slices. Dip the slices into the lemon water, then drain.
3   Put the fennel slices into a large food pouch. Add the oil and a little seasoning. Push the ingredients into a single, even layer and vacuum-seal.
4   When at temperature, put the pouch into the water bath. Put the rack horizontally on top of the pouch to keep it submerged. Cover with the lid and cook for 1–2 hours.
5   Lift the pouch from the water bath and remove the fennel slices. Pat them dry with kitchen paper.
6   Heat a little oil and butter in a ridged frying pan and, when very hot, add the fennel slices. Cook quickly until browned on both sides and serve immediately.

At the end of step 4, the vacuum-sealed food pouch can be ice-chilled and refrigerated for up to four days.

Creamy Cauliflower Purée

Vegetable purées – with their smooth, silky texture – give a smart look to a plate of food. For elegance, swirl them onto a plate and arrange your piece of fish or meat, or vegetables, on top.

Serves: 2–4
Water bath cooking time: 2–2½ hours

1 cauliflower
2 tbsp unsalted butter
Salt and freshly milled white pepper
To finish the dish
150ml/¼ pint double cream

1   Fill the water bath and preheat to 84°C/183°F.
2   Trim the leaves and stalk from the cauliflower (you can use them in another recipe). Cut or break the cauliflower into small florets, then thoroughly wash and drain.
3   Put the cauliflower florets into a large food pouch. Add the butter and a little seasoning. Push the ingredients into a single, even layer and vacuum-seal.
4   When at temperature, put the pouch into the water bath. Put the rack horizontally on top of the pouch to keep it submerged. Cover with the lid and cook for 2–2½ hours.
5   To finish the dish, lift the pouch from the water bath. Transfer the cauliflower florets to a pan and pour over the cream. Use a stick blender to whizz the mixture until smooth. Heat until piping hot, season to taste and serve immediately.

At the end of step 4, the vacuum-sealed food pouch can be ice-chilled and refrigerated for up to four days.

Courgettes with Thai Dressing

This makes a great starter, or you could include as part of a mezze – a collection of small dishes to serve at a buffet.

Serves: 2–4
Water bath cooking time: 30–45 minutes

2–3 large courgettes
2 tbsp sunflower oil
Salt and freshly milled white pepper
To finish the dish
1 small piece of fresh lemongrass
1 spring onion
1 large handful of coriander leaves
6 tbsp sunflower oil
2 tbsp white wine vinegar
2 tsp Thai fish sauce

1   Fill the water bath and preheat to 84°C/183°F.
2   Trim the courgettes and cut into bite-sized pieces.
3   Put the courgette pieces into a large food pouch. Add the oil and a little seasoning. Push the ingredients into a single, even layer and vacuum-seal.
4   When at temperature, put the pouch into the water bath. Put the rack horizontally on top of the pouch to keep it submerged. Cover with the lid and cook for 30–45 minutes.
5   To finish the dish, finely chop the lemongrass, spring onion and coriander leaves. Pour the oil, vinegar and fish sauce into a bowl and whisk together, then stir in the chopped ingredients. Season to taste, cover and chill until needed.
6   Lift the pouch from the water bath. Remove the pieces of courgette and arrange on a wide shallow dish. Spoon over the marinade, cover and chill for 2 hours before serving, carefully turning the courgettes in the marinade once or twice.

Spice-crusted Potatoes

Mustard, cumin and sesame seeds add bags of flavour to this dish.

Serves: 2–4
Water bath cooking time: 45 minutes–1½ hours

4 potatoes, each about 175g/6oz
4 tsp vegetable oil
Salt and freshly milled black pepper
To finish the dish
1 large handful of coriander leaves
1 tbsp mustard seeds
1 tbsp sesame seeds
2 tsp cumin seeds
2 tbsp vegetable oil
Thick natural yogurt, to serve

1   Fill the water bath and preheat to 84°C/183°F.
2   Scrub the potatoes but do not peel them. Cut them into bite-sized pieces.
3   Put the potato pieces into four food pouches. Add the oil and a little seasoning, then shake the pouch to mix the ingredients. Push the ingredients into a single, even layer and vacuum-seal.
4   When at temperature, put the pouches into the pouch holder and lower into the water bath. Cover with the lid and cook for 45 minutes.
5   Lift the pouch from the water bath and, wearing oven gloves, gently squeeze a piece of potato to see if it's cooked. The potato needs to be tender but still hold its shape. If necessary, return the pouch to the water bath for up to a further 45 minutes until the potato is tender.
6   To finish the dish, chop the coriander leaves. Lightly crush the mustard, sesame and cumin seeds. Lift the pouches from the water bath. Remove the potato pieces and place them to dry a little on a tray lined with kitchen paper.
7   Heat the oil in a wide, shallow pan, preferably non-stick, then stir in the crushed mustard, sesame and cumin seeds and turn them in the oil for 2–3 seconds. Add the potatoes, carefully turning them in the hot mix until golden and piping hot. Season to taste and scatter the coriander over the dish. Serve with thick yogurt.

At the end of step 4, the vacuum-sealed food pouches can be ice-chilled and refrigerated for up to four days.

Corn-on-the-Cob with Lemon and Parsley Butter

Buy fresh cobs that are heavy for their size, as they will be the freshest and tastiest. For a touch of heat, I sometimes add a little chilli paste to the parsley butter.

Serves: 2
Water bath cooking time: 45 minutes–1½ hours

2 corn on the cobs
1 small handful of parsley leaves
2 tbsp unsalted butter
To finish the dish
Salt and freshly milled black pepper

1   Fill the water bath and preheat to 84°C/183°F.
2   Pull any husks and silky threads from the cobs. Finely chop the parsley and put this into a small bowl with the butter. Mix until softened.
3   Spread the parsley butter over the corn-on-the-cobs. Put them into a large food pouch and vacuum-seal.
4   When at temperature, put the pouch into the water bath. Put the rack horizontally on top of the pouch to keep it submerged. Cover with the lid and cook for 45 minutes–1½ hours.
5   Lift the pouch from the water bath and remove the cobs. Season to taste and serve immediately.

Spiced Beetroots and Cranberries with Sesame Seeds

This is a dish of vivid colours. I always wear disposable gloves when handling beetroots, otherwise they will discolour your hands.

Serves: 2–4
Water bath cooking time: 2–4 hours

4 medium beetroots
1 red onion
1 small handful of cranberries, thawed if frozen
1 tbsp lemon juice
2 tbsp vegetable stock
¼ tsp ground cumin
¼ tsp ground ginger
Salt and freshly milled black pepper
To finish the dish
2 tbsp toasted sesame seeds

1   Fill the water bath and preheat to 84°C/183°F.
2   Trim any stalks from the beetroots and remove the skins using a potato peeler. Cut them into bite-sized pieces. Finely chop the onion and halve the cranberries.
3   Pour the lemon juice and stock into a small bowl and mix in the ground cumin, ginger and a little seasoning.
4   Put the beetroots, onion and cranberries into a large pouch and pour in the spice mix. Massage the pouch to mix the ingredients together. Push into a single, even layer and vacuum-seal.
5   When at temperature, put the pouch into the water bath. Put the rack horizontally on top of the pouch to keep it submerged. Cover with the lid and cook for 2–4 hours.
6   To finish the dish, lift the pouch from the water bath. Pour any liquid into a small pan, bring to the boil and cook until reduced and thickened a little. Meanwhile, spoon the beetroot mixture into a hot dish. Pour the juice over the beetroot mixture, sprinkle the sesame seeds over the top and serve immediately.

At the end of step 5, the vacuum-sealed food pouch can be ice-chilled and refrigerated for up to four days, or frozen.

Cabbage with Onion and Soured Cream

This recipe also works really well when made with cauliflower or broccoli. Use a mild or strong mustard, as you prefer.

Serves: 2–4
Water bath cooking time: 45 minutes–1 hour

¼ small white cabbage, about 350g/12oz
2 tbsp unsalted butter
Salt and freshly milled black pepper
To finish the dish
1 red onion
1 tbsp vegetable oil
150ml/¼ pint soured cream
¼ tsp prepared English mustard
1 tbsp vegetable stock

1   Fill the water bath and preheat to 84°C/183°F.
2   Finely shred the cabbage, wash and drain.
3   Put the cabbage into a large food pouch, then add the butter and a little seasoning. Shake the pouch to mix the ingredients. Push the ingredients into a single, even layer and vacuum-seal.
4   When at temperature, put the pouch into the water bath. Put the rack horizontally on top of the pouch to keep it submerged. Cover with the lid and cook for 45 minutes–1 hour.
5   To finish the dish, finely chop the onion. Heat the oil and fry the onion until golden and cooked. Stir in the soured cream, mustard and stock. Bring just to the boil and season to taste.
6   Lift the pouch from the water bath. Remove and drain the cabbage, then stir the cabbage into the onion mixture and serve immediately.

At the end of step 4, the vacuum-sealed food pouch can be ice-chilled and refrigerated for up to four days, or frozen.

Squash with Lemon

Refreshingly sharp and a very simple dish to make, you can also try this with pumpkins when they are in season.

Serves: 2–4
Water bath cooking time: 1–2 hours

800g/1¾lb wedge of squash, such as butternut or acorn
2 tbsp butter
2 tsp lemon zest
Freshly milled black pepper
To finish the dish
Crème fraîche
Chopped chives

1   Fill the water bath and preheat to 84°C/183°F.
2   Peel and discard any seeds from the squash and cut into bite-sized pieces.
3   Put the prepared squash into a large food pouch. Add the butter, lemon zest and a little seasoning. Push the ingredients into a single, even layer and vacuum-seal.
4   When at temperature, put the pouch into the water bath. Put the rack horizontally on top of the pouch to keep it submerged. Cover with the lid and cook for 1-2 hours.
5   Lift the pouch from the water bath. Remove the vegetables and serve immediately.
6   To finish the dish, serve topped with a spoonful of crème fraîche and a scattering of chopped chives.

At the end of step 4, the vacuum-sealed food pouch can be ice-chilled and refrigerated for up to four days, or frozen.

Red Pepper and Sweet Potato Crush

Warm, orange-coloured sweet potato has sweetness and a hint of spice. It's perfectly partnered by the brightness and mild heat of red pepper.

Serves: 2–4
Water bath cooking time: 45 minutes–2 hours

2 sweet potatoes, about 500g/1lb 2oz total
1 red pepper
2 tbsp olive oil
Salt and freshly milled black pepper

1   Fill the water bath and preheat to 84°C/183°F.
2   Peel the sweet potatoes and cut into bite-sized pieces. Cut the red pepper in half, remove and discard the seeds and stalk, and finely chop.
3   Put the potato and red pepper pieces into a large food pouch and add the olive oil and a little seasoning. Shake the pouch to mix the ingredients. Push the ingredients into a single, even layer and vacuum-seal.
4   When at temperature, put the pouch into the water bath. Put the rack horizontally on top of the pouch to keep it submerged. Cover with the lid and cook for 45 minutes–2 hours until the sweet potato feels soft.
5   Lift the pouch from the water bath and massage the pouch lightly to crush the contents. Serve immediately.

At the end of step 4, the vacuum-sealed food pouch can be ice-chilled and refrigerated for up to four days.

Green Bean and Pancetta Salad

A salad with the flavours of Italy. Pancetta is an Italian cured bacon, usually unsmoked, and sold already diced. Alternatively, use thick-cut smoked or unsmoked bacon cut into small cubes.

Serves: 2–4
Water bath cooking time: 35 minutes–1 hour

350g/12oz French beans
280g/10oz broad beans
1 tbsp vegetable oil
Salt and freshly milled black pepper
To finish the dish
6 tbsp olive oil
2 tbsp red wine vinegar
1 tsp lemon juice
1 handful of chopped mixed herb leaves such as dill, tarragon, basil
250g/9oz pancetta pieces
A few sliced black olives
Parmesan shavings
Hot ciabatta bread, to serve

1   Fill the water bath and preheat to 84°C/183°F.
2   Trim the French beans and cut in half. To keep them a brighter green, put all the beans into a pan of boiling water for 10 seconds, then immediately drain and put into a bowl of iced water until cold. Drain and dry on kitchen paper.
3   Put the beans into a large food pouch and add the oil and a little seasoning. Shake the pouch to mix the ingredients. Push the ingredients into a single, even layer and vacuum-seal.
4   When at temperature, put the pouch into the water bath. Put the rack horizontally on top of the pouch to keep it submerged. Cover with the lid and cook for 35 minutes–1 hour.

5 To finish the dish, pour the oil, vinegar and lemon juice into a bowl and whisk together, then stir in the chopped herbs. Season to taste, cover and chill until needed.
6 Lift the pouch from the water bath, remove the beans and drain. Tip the beans into a bowl and stir in the dressing. Cover and chill until cold.
7 Just before serving, heat a non-stick pan and dry-fry the pancetta until browned and cooked through.
8 Stir the pancetta, some sliced olives and Parmesan shavings into the bean salad and serve immediately with hot ciabatta bread.

At the end of step 4, the vacuum-sealed food pouch can be ice-chilled and refrigerated for up to four days.

Brussels Sprouts and Chestnuts

I'm a great fan of brussels sprouts. There are new varieties now being grown that have a milder taste than the old varieties.

Serves: 2–4
Water bath cooking time: 45 minutes–1 hour

280g/10oz fresh brussels sprouts
1 tbsp unsalted butter
Salt and freshly milled black pepper
To finish the dish
6 cooked shelled chestnuts
2 tbsp unsalted butter
1 tbsp sunflower oil
1 tbsp grated orange rind

1   Fill the water bath and preheat to 84°C/183°F.
2   Trim the sprouts and remove any damaged leaves. To keep them a brighter green, put the sprouts into a pan of boiling water for 10 seconds, then immediately drain and put into a bowl of iced water until cold. Drain and dry on kitchen paper.
3   Put the sprouts into a large food pouch and add the butter and a little seasoning. Shake the pouch to mix the ingredients. Push the ingredients into a single, even layer and vacuum-seal.
4   When at temperature, put the pouch into the water bath. Put the rack horizontally on top of the pouch to keep it submerged. Cover with the lid and cook for 45 minutes–1 hour.
5   To finish the dish, halve the chestnuts. Lift the pouch from the water bath, remove the brussels sprouts and drain. Heat the butter and oil in a pan until hot, then stir in the brussels sprouts, chestnuts and orange rind and cook, stirring, until piping hot. Serve immediately.

At the end of step 4, the vacuum-sealed food pouch can be ice-chilled and refrigerated for up to four days, or frozen.

Sweet and Sour Red Cabbage

A bright colourful dish, full of interesting flavours and just a touch of sweetness.

Serves: 2–4
Water bath cooking time: 2–4 hours

¼ small red cabbage, about 350g/12oz
1 small red onion
1 small orange
2 tbsp clear honey
1 tbsp red wine vinegar
1 tbsp vegetable stock
1 tbsp vegetable oil
Salt and freshly milled black pepper

1   Fill the water bath and preheat to 84°C/183°F.
2   Finely shred the cabbage and chop the onion. Zest the orange, cut in half and squeeze out the juices.
3   Pour the orange juice, honey and vinegar into a non-metallic bowl and mix in the stock, oil and a little seasoning. Add the cabbage and onion and stir until coated.
4   Put the vegetable mix into two food pouches. Push the ingredients into a single, even layer and vacuum-seal.
5   When at temperature, put the pouches into the pouch holder and lower into the water bath. Cover with the lid and cook for 2–4 hours.
6   To finish the dish, lift the pouches from the water bath. Pour the liquid into a wide pan, bring to the boil and cook until reduced and thickened a little. Stir in the red cabbage mixture to coat in the sauce, then serve immediately.

At the end of step 5, the vacuum-sealed food pouches can be ice-chilled and refrigerated for up to four days, or frozen.

Cavolo Nero

Cavolo nero is a type of Italian cabbage, not actually black, as the name suggests, but with very dark green leaves. As darker green vegetables sometimes lose a little colour when cooked, it's worth blanching and icing the cabbage first to help preserve the colour.

Serves: 2–4
Water bath cooking time: 30 minutes–1 hour

6 cavolo nero leaves
2 tbsp unsalted butter
Salt and freshly milled black pepper

1   Fill the water bath and preheat to 84°C/183°F
2   Shred the cavolo nero leaves. To keep it a brighter green, put the cavolo nero into a pan of boiling water for 10 seconds, then immediately drain and put into a bowl of iced water until cold. Drain and dry on kitchen paper.
3   Put the cavolo nero into a large food pouch. Add the butter and a little seasoning. Push the ingredients into a single, even layer and vacuum-seal.
4   When at temperature, put the pouch into the water bath. Put the rack horizontally on top of the pouch to keep it submerged. Cover with the lid and cook for 30 minutes–1 hour.
5   Lift the pouch from the water bath, remove the cavolo nero and serve immediately.

At the end of step 4, the vacuum-sealed food pouch can be ice-chilled and refrigerated for up to four days.

Shallots with Wholegrain Mustard

A useful vegetable accompaniment to serve with meat and poultry, shallots have a slightly sweeter flavour than onions.

Serves: 4–6
Water bath cooking time: 2–4 hours

450g/1lb shallots
2 tbsp vegetable stock
To finish the dish
Oil and butter, for frying
2 tbsp wholegrain mustard
Salt and freshly milled black pepper

1   Fill the water bath and preheat to 84°C/183°F.
2   Trim the stems and roots of the shallots and peel off the outer layer of skin. Cut in half lengthways.
3   Put the shallots and stock into two food pouches. Push the ingredients into a single, even layer and vacuum-seal.
4   When at temperature, put the pouches into the pouch holder and lower into the water bath. Cover with the lid and cook for 2–4 hours.
5   To finish the dish, lift the pouches from the water bath, remove the shallots and dry on kitchen paper. Heat a little oil and butter in a frying pan and cook the shallots until they begin to brown. Stir in the wholegrain mustard and a little seasoning; then serve piping hot.

At the end of step 4, the vacuum-sealed food pouches can be ice-chilled and refrigerated for up to four days.

2

Fish and Shellfish

It's good to opt for fish on a regular basis with any healthy eating plan, and there is such a variety of fish available that turning them into delicious, appetizing meals using your sous vide need never be a problem. There are distinctive ways of preparing fish in readiness for the pouches and the water bath, but there is no need to make things complicated. With sous vide home cooking in mind, I have designed this range of recipes to be simple and straightforward. The results, however, will be anything but simple, with all those wonderful fishy flavours and textures being brought to finesse in the finished meals.

When cooking fish and shellfish sous vide remember to:
• Buy very fresh fish or shellfish.
• If possible, use fish from sustainable sources.
• Keep it chilled until you are ready to use it.
• Make sure any visible bones are removed with tweezers as they may puncture the pouch.
• When vacuum-sealing the pouch, don't over-pulse as this may crush the fish or shellfish.
• Remember when browning fish or shellfish – in a pan, under the grill or with a culinary blow torch – to do it quickly because the food will continue to cook.
• Cooking times relate to fish fillets and shellfish having a thickness of 1–2.5cm/½–1in, or being bite-sized.

Zesty Salmon with Orange and Fennel

A warm salad that is light, fresh and full of flavour. This would go well with Charred Fennel (see page 13).

Serves: 4
Water bath cooking time: 40–50 minutes

4 x 175g/6oz skinless salmon fillets
4 tbsp unsalted butter
4 lemon slices
4 sprigs of fennel
Salt and freshly milled black pepper
To finish the dish
1 small orange
1 small lemon
1 small handful of fennel leaves
A few walnut halves
4 tbsp olive oil
½ tsp Dijon mustard
Pinch of sugar
Salad leaves, to serve

1   Fill the water bath and preheat to 60°C/140°F.
2   Remove any visible bones from the salmon fillets with tweezers.
3   Put the fillets into four food pouches. Add a tablespoon of butter, a lemon slice, a fennel sprig and a little seasoning to each pouch and vacuum-seal.
4   When at temperature, put the pouches into the pouch rack and lower into the water bath, cover with the lid and cook for 40–50 minutes.
5   To finish the dish, zest or finely grate the orange and lemon. Cut both in half and squeeze out all the juices. Finely chop the fennel leaves and the walnuts.

6 Pour the orange and lemon zest and juices into a small pan over a low heat for a few minutes until the zest has softened and the juice reduced a little. Cool a little and pour into a bowl with the oil, mustard and sugar. Whisk together, stir in the fennel leaves and walnuts and season to taste.

7 Lift the pouches from the water bath. Transfer the salmon fillets to plates and spoon over the dressing. Serve warm with salad leaves.

At the end of step 4, the vacuum-sealed food pouches can be ice-chilled and refrigerated for up to three days, or frozen.

Trout with Couscous

With a Moroccan influence to this dish, the lovely grainy texture of the couscous absorbs all the wonderful flavours.

Serves: 2
Water bath cooking time: 40–50 minutes

2 x 175g/6oz trout fillets
2 tbsp unsalted butter
2 lemon slices
Salt and freshly milled black pepper
To finish the dish
175g/6oz couscous
1 red onion
1 red chilli
3 ready-to-eat dried apricots
1 handful of coriander leaves
3 tbsp sunflower oil
150ml/¼ pint chicken stock
1 small handful of sultanas
Lemon wedges, to serve

1   Fill the water bath and preheat to 60°C/140°F.
2   Remove any visible bones from the trout fillets with tweezers.
3   Put the fillets into two food pouches. Divide the butter between them, add a lemon slice and a little seasoning to each one and vacuum-seal.
4   When at temperature, put the pouches into the pouch rack and lower into the water bath, cover with the lid and cook for 40–50 minutes.
5   To finish the dish, put the couscous into a large bowl and pour over enough boiling water to cover. Leave to stand, stirring occasionally. Finely chop the onion. Cut the chilli in half, remove the seeds and stalk and finely chop. Thinly slice the apricots and chop the coriander.

7 Heat 2 tbsp of oil in a non-stick pan. Add the onion and chilli and cook for about 5 minutes until softened. Stir in the stock, apricots, sultanas and half the chopped coriander. Season to taste. Bring just to the boil and cook for 10 minutes.

8 Drain the couscous and stir it into the onion mixture. Cook, stirring, for 3 minutes until the couscous is piping hot. Stir in the remaining chopped coriander and season to taste.

9 When ready to serve, lift the pouches from the water bath and remove the trout. Pat them dry with kitchen paper. Brush with the remaining oil and put under a hot grill for a few seconds to brown and crisp the skin, or use a culinary blow torch.

10 Pile the couscous onto plates and put the trout fillets on top, skin-side up, and serve immediately with lemon wedges.

At the end of step 4, the vacuum-sealed food pouches can be ice-chilled and refrigerated for up to two days, or frozen.

33

Parma Ham-wrapped Monkfish with Mushrooms

Monkfish has a firm, meaty texture that is perfect for the elegant surf-and-turf combination in this recipe.

Serves: 2
Water bath cooking time: 40–50 minutes

4 slices Parma ham
2 x 175g/6oz skinless monkfish fillets
Salt and freshly milled black pepper
To finish the dish
250g/9oz mixed mushrooms, such as shiitake, chestnut, oyster
2 tbsp butter
250ml/9fl oz chicken stock
1½ tbsp balsamic vinegar
1 tsp sugar
2 tsp lemon juice
2 tbsp freshly chopped parsley
Oil, for frying

1   Fill the water bath and preheat to 60°C/140°F.
2   Wrap two slices of ham around each fish fillet and put the fillets into two food pouches. Add a little seasoning and vacuum-seal.
3   When at temperature, put the pouches into the pouch rack and lower into the water bath, cover with the lid and cook for 40–50 minutes.
4   To finish the dish, clean and trim the mushrooms and slice thickly.
5   Heat the butter in a pan and cook the mushrooms for about 5 minutes until golden. Add the stock, vinegar, sugar and lemon juice, bring to the boil, then cook gently until the liquid has reduced by half. Stir in the chopped parsley and season to taste.
6   When ready to serve, lift the pouches from the water bath and remove the monkfish. Pat them dry with kitchen paper. Heat a little oil in a frying pan until very hot. Quickly turn the fish in the pan for a few seconds to brown and crisp the ham, or use a culinary blow torch. Thickly slice each fillet and serve immediately with the mushrooms.

At the end of step 3, the vacuum-sealed food pouches can be ice-chilled and refrigerated for up to three days, or frozen.

Smoked Haddock with Savoury Rice

This recipe also works well with whiting or salmon but, whatever fish I use, I always prefer to use undyed.

Serves: 4
Water bath cooking time: 40–50 minutes

3 x 175g/6oz undyed, skinless smoked haddock fillets
3 tbsp butter
Salt and freshly milled black pepper
To finish the dish
1 red onion
1 lime
1 small bunch of flat-leaf parsley
1 small bunch of chives
2 tbsp sunflower oil
1 handful of peas
150ml/¼ pint vegetable or fish stock
250g/9oz cooked long-grain rice

1   Fill the water bath and preheat to 60°C/140°F.
2   Remove any visible bones from the haddock fillets with tweezers.
3   Put the fillets into three food pouches. Add some butter and a little seasoning to each one and vacuum-seal.
4   When at temperature, put the pouches into the pouch rack and lower into the water bath, cover with the lid and cook for 40–50 minutes.
5   To finish the dish, finely chop the onion. Grate the rind from half the lime, cut the lime in half and squeeze the juice from both halves. Finely chop the parsley and chives.
6   Heat the oil in a non-stick frying pan, add the onion and cook until it is beginning to brown. Stir in the peas, grated lime, lime juice, vegetable or fish stock and half the chopped parsley and chives. Bring just to the boil, then cook for 5 minutes. Stir in the rice and cook until piping hot.
7   Lift the pouches from the water bath and remove the haddock fillets. Flake the fish, then stir it into the rice mixture with the remaining parsley and chives. Season to taste and serve immediately.

At the end of step 4, the vacuum-sealed food pouches can be ice-chilled and refrigerated for up to two days, or frozen.

Fish Cakes

Fishmongers usually sell a mixed fish selection of small pieces that work well in many dishes such as this one. I like the way the extra flavours work together.

Serves: 4
Water bath cooking time: 40–50 minutes

350g/12oz mixed skinless fish pieces such as smoked haddock, whiting, salmon, plaice or trout
2 tbsp butter
2 lemon slices
Salt and freshly milled black pepper
To finish the dish
2 spring onions
1 small handful of flat-leaf parsley
350g/12oz cooked mashed potatoes
3 tbsp polenta
Oil, for frying
Chips, peas and lemon wedges, to serve

1   Fill the water bath and preheat to 60°C/140°F.
2   Remove any visible bones from the fish pieces with tweezers. Put the fish pieces into two food pouches. Add some butter, a lemon slice, and a little seasoning to each and vacuum-seal.
3   When at temperature, put the pouches into the pouch rack and lower into the water bath, cover with the lid and cook for 40–50 minutes.
4   To finish the dish, lift the pouches from the water bath and remove the fish pieces. Flake the fish, removing any bones. Finely chop the spring onions and the parsley.
5   Put the mashed potato into a bowl and mix in the chopped onions and parsley, and the flaked fish. Season to taste.
6   Run your hands under the tap to dampen them, then shape the mixture into eight balls and flatten each one into a disc. Tip the polenta onto a plate, then roll the balls in the polenta until coated.
7   Heat a little oil in the frying pan, add the fish cakes and cook until browned on both sides, cooked through and piping hot.
8   Serve immediately with chips, peas and lemon wedges.

At the end of step 3, the vacuum-sealed food pouches can be ice-chilled and refrigerated for up to three days, or frozen.

Mediterranean Tuna

I have combined the classic Mediterranean flavours – anchovies, olives, capers, basil and tomatoes – in this summer dish.

Serves: 2
Water bath cooking time: 40–50 minutes

2 x 175g/6oz skinless tuna steaks, about 1–2.5cm/½–1in thick
1 tbsp sunflower oil
Salt and freshly milled black pepper
To finish the dish
1 courgette
1 small onion
8 cherry tomatoes
6 stoned black olives
4 anchovy fillets
2 tbsp sunflower oil
2 tbsp capers
150ml/¼ pint vegetable stock
1 tbsp toasted pine nuts
1 handful of basil leaves
Lemon wedges, to serve

1   Fill the water bath and preheat to 60°C/140°F.
2   Put the tuna steaks into two food pouches. Add some oil and a little seasoning and vacuum-seal.
3   When at temperature, put the pouches into the pouch rack and lower into the water bath, cover with the lid and cook for 40–50 minutes.
4   To finish the dish, coarsely grate the courgette and thinly slice the onion. Halve the tomatoes and olives. Roughly chop the anchovy fillets.
5   Heat the oil in a pan, add the onion and cook until softened. Stir in the chopped anchovies and cook for 2–3 minutes until they begin to dissolve. Add the grated courgette, tomatoes, olives, capers and stock. Bring just to the boil, then cook for 10 minutes, stirring occasionally. Stir in the pine nuts and basil leaves and season to taste.
6   Lift the pouches from the water bath and remove the tuna steaks.
7   Serve the tuna with the courgette mixture spooned over and some lemon wedges on the side.

At the end of step 3, the vacuum-sealed food pouches can be ice-chilled and refrigerated for up to two days, or frozen.

Sea Bass with Watercress and Cucumber Dressing

The skin is left on the sea bass so it can be browned and crisped under the grill or with a culinary blow torch.

Serves: 2
Water bath cooking time: 40–50 minutes

2x 175g/6oz sea bass fillets
2 tbsp unsalted butter
2 lime slices
Salt and freshly milled black pepper
To finish the dish
1 small cucumber
1 bunch of watercress
2 spring onions
3 tbsp sunflower oil
1 tbsp cider vinegar
1 tbsp lime juice
1 tsp grated ginger
Oil, for brushing

1   Fill the water bath and preheat to 60°C/140°F.
2   Remove any visible bones from the sea bass fillets with tweezers.
3   Put the fillets into two food pouches. Add some butter, a lime slice and a little seasoning and vacuum-seal.
4   When at temperature, put the pouches into the pouch rack and lower into the water bath, cover with the lid and cook for 40-50 minutes.
5   To finish the dish, cut the cucumber in half lengthwise. Scoop out and discard the seeds. Roughly chop the cucumber. Put it into a sieve over a bowl and sprinkle some salt over – this will draw out some of the liquid. Leave for an hour then wash away the salt and dry the cucumber on kitchen paper. Pull the leaves from the watercress stalks and cut the spring onions into four pieces.

6   Pour the sunflower oil, vinegar and lime juice into a food processor. Add the cucumber, watercress, spring onions and ginger and process until smooth. Season to taste.

7   When ready to serve, lift the pouches from the water bath and remove the sea bass. Pat them dry with kitchen paper. Brush with a little oil and put under a hot grill for a few seconds to brown and crisp the skin, or use a culinary blow torch.

8   Serve the sea bass fillets, skin side uppermost, with the cucumber and watercress dressing.

At the end of step 4, the vacuum-sealed food pouches can be ice-chilled and refrigerated for up to three days, or frozen.

Coconut Fish Curry

A delicious light fresh curry for which you can choose your preferred strength of curry powder. If available, add a tablespoon or two of freshly grated coconut.

Serves: 4
Water bath cooking time: 40–50 minutes

500g/1lb 2oz mixed skinless fish pieces such as smoked haddock, whiting, salmon, plaice or trout
Salt and freshly milled black pepper
To finish the dish
1 onion
250g/9oz French beans
2 tbsp vegetable oil
2 tbsp curry powder
1 tsp ground cumin
1 tsp ground coriander
300ml/½ pint chicken stock
400g can coconut milk
100g bag baby spinach leaves
Naan bread and pickles, to serve

1 Fill the water bath and preheat to 60°C/140°F.
2 Remove any visible bones from the fish pieces with tweezers and cut into bite-sized pieces.
3 Put the fish into two food pouches and add a little seasoning. Push the ingredients into a single, even layer and vacuum-seal.
4 When at temperature, put the pouches into the pouch rack and lower into the water bath, cover with the lid and cook for 40–50 minutes.
5 To finish the dish, finely chop the onion. Cut the beans into short lengths.

6   Heat the oil in a pan and fry the onion until softened but not browned. Stir in the curry powder, ground cumin and ground coriander, then cook for a minute. Pour in the stock, coconut milk and add a little seasoning. Bring to the boil and cook for 15 minutes. Add the beans and spinach and cook until the beans are tender. Season to taste.

7   When ready to serve lift the pouches from the water bath. Remove the fish pieces and add to the curry mixture. Carefully stir the fish into the curry and season to taste.

8   Serve immediately with warm naan bread and pickles.

At the end of step 4, the vacuum-sealed food pouches can be ice-chilled and refrigerated for up to three days, or frozen.

Fish Soup

A soup packed with flavour, which would work as well with just one or two types of fish.

Serves: 2–4
Water bath cooking time: 40–50 minutes

1 red onion
2 garlic cloves
1 tbsp sunflower oil
250g/9oz mixed skinless fish pieces such as smoked haddock, whiting, salmon, plaice or trout
2 tbsp vegetable stock
½ tsp dried mixed herbs
Salt and freshly ground black pepper
To finish the dish
150ml/¼ pint fish or vegetable stock
2 tbsp tomato purée
200g can tomatoes
4 tbsp chopped parsley
Hot crusty bread, to serve

1 Finely chop the onion and garlic.
2 Heat the oil in a pan, add the chopped onion and garlic and cook until lightly browned and softened. Put the softened vegetables into a bowl, chill and refrigerate until cold.
3 Fill the water bath and preheat to 60°C/140°F.
4 Remove any visible bones from the fish pieces with tweezers and cut into bite-sized pieces.
5 Put the fish into a large food pouch and add the onion mixture, stock, mixed herbs and a little seasoning. Shake the pouch to mix the ingredients. Push the ingredients into a single, even layer and vacuum-seal.
6 When at temperature, put the pouch into the water bath. Put the rack horizontally on top of the pouch to keep it submerged. Cover with the lid and cook for 40–50 minutes.

7   To finish the dish, pour the stock into a pan and add the tomato purée and tomatoes. Bring just to the boil and cook for 15 minutes.

8   Lift the pouch from the water bath and pour the contents into the tomato mixture in the pan. Use a stick blender to whizz the soup to the consistency you prefer — chunky or smooth. Stir in the parsley and season to taste.

9   Serve immediately with hot crusty bread.

At the end of step 6, the vacuum-sealed food pouch can be ice-chilled and refrigerated for up to two days, or frozen.

Ginger and Lemon Prawns

A tangy, slightly spicy treatment for ever-popular prawns, you could also serve the prawns with wraps.

Serves: 2
Water bath cooking time: 30–40 minutes

250g/9oz shelled raw prawns
1 tbsp sunflower oil
1 tsp grated fresh ginger
2 tsp lemon zest
Salt and freshly milled black pepper
To finish the dish
Hot pancakes, wraps or flour tortillas
Salad leaves and salad dressing, to serve

1   Fill the water bath and preheat to 60°C/140°F.
2   If the prawns haven't been de-veined, then with a sharp knife make a slit along the back of the prawns. Pull out the black digestive tract that is just below the surface. Rinse the prawns in cold water, drain and dry on kitchen paper.
3   In a bowl, mix together the sunflower oil, grated ginger, lemon zest and a little seasoning. Gently stir the prawns into the mixture until thoroughly coated.
4   Spoon the coated prawns and any excess dressing into two food pouches. Push them into a single, even layer and vacuum-seal.
5   When at temperature, put the pouches into the pouch rack and lower into the water bath, cover with the lid and cook for 30–40 minutes.
6   To finish the dish, lift the pouches from the water bath and remove the prawn mixture.
7   Serve immediately with hot pancakes and salad, or try with wraps or flour tortillas.

At the end of step 4, the vacuum-sealed food pouches can be ice-chilled and refrigerated for up to three days.

Prawns with Fennel and Almonds

Prawns with a nutty, crunchy topping and a hint of aniseed.

Serves: 2
Water bath cooking time: 30–40 minutes

250g/9oz shelled raw prawns
4 sprigs of fennel
Salt and freshly milled black pepper
To finish the dish
3 tbsp chopped almonds
2 tbsp Parmesan cheese
Hot garlic bread and watercress leaves, to serve

1   Fill the water bath and preheat to 60°C/140°F.
2   If the prawns haven't been de-veined, then with a sharp knife make a slit along the back of the prawns. Pull out the black digestive tract that is just below the surface. Rinse the prawns in cold water, drain and dry on kitchen paper. Finely chop the fennel sprigs.
3   Put the prawns into two food pouches and add the chopped fennel and a little seasoning. Push them into a single, even layer and vacuum-seal.
4   When at temperature, put the pouches into the pouch rack and lower into the water bath, cover with the lid and cook for 30–40 minutes.
5   To finish the dish, in a bowl mix together the chopped almonds, Parmesan cheese and a little seasoning. Lift the pouches from the water bath. Remove the prawns and put them into two heated, flameproof dishes. Thinly scatter over the almond mixture and put under a hot grill until the cheese has melted, or use a culinary blow torch.
6   Serve immediately with hot garlic bread and watercress leaves.

At the end of step 4, the vacuum-sealed food pouches can be ice-chilled and refrigerated for up to two days.

Scallops with Samphire

Samphire is a salty tangy vegetable, more widely available these days in fishmongers and supermarkets.

Serves: 2
Water bath cooking time: 30–40 minutes

6 scallops
To finish the dish
2 large handfuls of samphire
1 tbsp butter
Salt and freshly milled black pepper
Vegetable oil, for frying
3 tbsp freshly chopped parsley
Lemon wedges, to serve

1   Fill the water bath and preheat to 60°C/140°F.
2   Wash the scallops in cold water and dry on kitchen paper
3   Arrange the scallops in two food pouches so they don't touch (see below) and vacuum-seal.
4   When at temperature, put the pouches into the pouch rack and lower into the water bath, cover with the lid and cook for 30–40 minutes.
5   To finish the dish, wash the samphire, discarding any 'woody' pieces. Cook in boiling water for 10 minutes and drain. Stir in the butter and a little seasoning, then heat until piping hot.
6   Lift the pouches from the water bath, remove the scallops and dry on kitchen paper. Heat a little oil in a frying pan and when hot quickly sear the scallops until golden brown on both sides.
7   Spoon the samphire into hot bowls. Add the scallops, sprinkle over the chopped parsley, drizzle a little of the cooking juices over the scallops and serve immediately with lemon wedges.

At the end of step 4 vacuum-sealed food pouches can be ice-chilled and refrigerated for up to two days.

To stop the scallops from touching, lay the pouch flat on the work surface, opened at one end. Slide solid food items into the bag, spaced out a little. The open end of the pouch is slid into the vacuum-sealing machine. As the air is sucked out of the bag from around each piece of scallop (or meatball, fritter or drumstick etc.) it leaves them in their own pocket.

3
Beef

Slow tenderising is the hallmark of cooking beef in the sous vide. We've all heard about the merits of slow cooking as a traditional technique for getting the best out of meat. With your high-tech, contemporary sous vide you can follow these familiar yet rather different recipes for delicious melt-in-the-mouth steaks, roasts and casseroles. After a long immersion in the water bath, the beef will emerge beautifully tenderized and moist, ready to satisfy the keenest appetite. Sample the mouth-watering recipe for Beef in Red Wine with Chestnuts (see page 50), and look out, too, for my take on that perennial favourite the beef burger, Herby Beef Burgers (see page 60) – this one infused with lovely mixed herbs.

When cooking beef sous vide remember to:
- Buy good-quality meat.
- Keep it chilled until ready to use.
- When putting meat into a sous vide pouch, fold back the top flap of the pouch. It's then easy to slide in the ingredients without them touching the outside of the pouch.
- Alcohol gives a metallic flavour to foods cooked sous vide. To avoid this, pour into a small pan and heat on the hob for a few minutes to drive off the alcohol.
- Salt can begin to cure the meat when longer cooking times are used, so I salt when the meat comes out of the water bath.
- Joints, chops or ribs with a bone in them may puncture the pouch, so avoid over-pulsing.
- Liquids such as stock or wine may be drawn out of the pouch when vacuum-sealing, so don't over-pulse. I often freeze them in ice cube trays and drop a cube or two into the pouch instead.
- Sear or brown meat very quickly, as the meat continues to cook during this process.
- Sous vide cooked beef needs only a few minutes resting time, rather than the longer time required with conventional cooking.

Rump Steak with Mushrooms and Horseradish

A moist, tender steak topped with a garlicky mushroom mix, as well as a kick of horseradish – delicious!

Serves: 2
Water bath cooking time: 2.5cm/1in thick, 1–4 hours; 5cm/2in thick, 2 –4 hours

2 x 175g/6oz rump steaks
Freshly milled black pepper
1 tsp vegetable oil
To finish the dish
1 shallot
1 garlic clove
1 courgette
1 large handful of button mushrooms
2 tbsp butter
Oil, for frying
300ml/½ pint beef stock
2 tsp lemon juice
½–1 tsp horseradish sauce
1 tbsp freshly chopped parsley
Salt and freshly milled black pepper

1 Fill the water bath and preheat to 60°C/140°F.
2 Trim the steaks and pat dry with kitchen paper.
3 Put each steak into a food pouch. Add a little pepper and oil and vacuum-seal.
4 When at temperature, put the pouches into the pouch rack and lower into the water bath, cover with the lid and cook for 1–4 hours (see timings above).
5 To finish the dish, finely chop the shallot. Crush and chop the garlic and finely chop the courgette. Clean and trim the mushrooms and halve.
6 Heat the butter and 1 tbsp of the oil in a pan and cook the shallot until softened and beginning to brown. Add the garlic, chopped courgette and mushroom halves, then cook until golden.

7   Stir in the stock, lemon juice and horseradish sauce to taste. Bring just to the boil and cook for 12–15 minutes. Stir in the chopped parsley and season to taste.

8   Lift the pouches from the water bath. Remove the steaks, dry on kitchen paper and season, if needed.

9   Heat a little oil in a heavy-based frying pan until very hot, add the steaks and quickly sear until browned on both sides, or brush with a little oil and use a culinary blow torch.

10 Serve the steaks with the mushroom mix.

At the end of step 4, the vacuum-sealed food pouches can be ice-chilled and refrigerated for up to four days, or frozen.

Beef in Red Wine with Chestnuts

Alcohol can give a metallic flavour to foods cooked sous vide unless you gently heat the wine in a pan to burn off the alcohol.

Serves: 4
Water bath cooking time: 12–14 hours

150ml/¼ pint red wine or unsweetened red grape juice
500g/1lb 2oz lean braising beef
1 tbsp vegetable oil
1 tsp dried thyme
1 tsp dried sage
To finish the dish
2 onions
1 small handful of cooked, peeled chestnuts, canned or frozen
2 sprigs of thyme leaves
2 tbsp vegetable oil
150ml/¼ pint red wine or unsweetened red grape juice
150ml/¼ pint beef stock
Salt and freshly milled black pepper
Rice and wilted spinach, to serve

1 Pour the red wine into a small pan and heat for a few minutes to drive off the alcohol. Pour into a small bowl and chill, ice and refrigerate until cold.
2 Fill the water bath and preheat to 60°C/140°F.
3 Trim any fat from the beef and cut into bite-sized pieces.
4 Heat a little oil in a heavy-based pan until very hot. Add the beef and quickly sear the meat on all sides — you may need to do this in batches. Pat dry with kitchen paper. (If not using immediately, remove and drain the meat, ice and refrigerate until cold.)
5 Put the beef into two pouches and add a little thyme, sage and wine to each. Push into a single, even layer and vacuum-seal, stopping before the liquid is drawn out of the bag.
6 When at temperature, put the pouches into the pouch holder and lower into the water bath, cover with the lid and cook for 12–14 hours.

7   To finish the dish, thinly slice the onions. Halve the chestnuts and pull the thyme leaves from the stalks.

8   Heat the oil in a large pan and cook the onions until lightly browned. Add the thyme leaves, chestnuts, red wine or grape juice, stock and seasoning. Bring to the boil and cook for 15 minutes until reduced.

9   Lift the pouches from the water bath. Snip the corner of each pouch and pour the juices into the pan. Stand the pouches back in the water bath keeping them upright so water doesn't get in (add a bag clip if you prefer) to keep the beef at temperature. Don't put the lid on the water bath. Bring the sauce with the additional juices to the boil once again and reduce as before.

10 Stir the beef into the hot sauce and serve with rice and wilted spinach.

At the end of step 6, the vacuum-sealed food pouches can be ice-chilled and refrigerated for up to four days, or frozen.

Rib Roast

A classic cut of meat given a tasty sticky crust.

Serves: 4–6
Water bath cooking time: 6–10 hours for medium rare

1.3 kg/3lb boneless rib beef roasting joint
1 tsp freshly milled black pepper
2 tsp ground thyme
To finish the dish
2 tsp ground thyme
2 tsp vegetable oil
2 tbsp Worcestershire sauce
3 tbsp clear honey
Salt and freshly milled black pepper
4 tsp horseradish sauce
150ml/¼ pint crème fraîche
Creamy Cauliflower Purée (see page 14), to serve

1   Fill the water bath and preheat to 60°C/140°F.
2   Trim the joint and pat dry with kitchen paper. Rub the pepper and thyme over the meat.
3   Put the beef joint into a large food pouch and vacuum-seal.
4   When at temperature, put the pouch into the water bath, cover with the lid and cook for 6–10 hours.
5   To finish the dish, heat the oven to 220°C/205°C fan/gas 7.
6   In a small bowl, mix together the ground thyme, oil, Worcestershire sauce and honey to form a paste. Season to taste with pepper and salt.
7   In another bowl mix together the horseradish sauce and crème fraîche for a dressing.

8 Lift the pouch from the water bath and remove the beef. Pat dry with kitchen paper and put it into a roasting tin.

9 Spread the paste over the beef. Put into a hot oven for about 6–8 minutes until the crust is golden. Alternatively use a culinary blow torch.

10 Remove the rib roast from the oven, carve into slices and serve with cauliflower purée and the horseradish dressing.

At the end of step 4, the vacuum-sealed food pouch can be ice-chilled and refrigerated for up to four days, or frozen.

Shredded Beef Tortillas

Shredded or 'pulled' beef is also very more-ish served in hot toasted sourdough sandwiches, in hot noodles or in rice.

Serves: 4–6
Water bath cooking time: 12–14 hours

700g/1lb 9oz boned joint of brisket
1–2 tsp ground fennel
To finish the dish
1 red onion
1 avocado
2 tsp lemon juice
Salt and freshly milled black pepper
Oil, for frying
Soft flour tortilla wraps
Baby spinach leaves
Rocket leaves
Soured cream
Chilli sauce (optional)

1   Fill the water bath and preheat to 60°C/140°F.
2   If the brisket is a rolled joint, remove any string ties, unroll and flatten out. With a sharp knife, score criss-cross lines through the fat. Pat dry with kitchen paper and rub the ground fennel all over the meat.
3   Put the brisket into a large pouch and vacuum-seal.
4   When at temperature, put the pouch into the water bath, cover with the lid and cook for 12–14 hours.
5   To finish the dish, thinly slice the onion. Cut the avocado in half, remove the stone and scoop out the flesh. Roughly chop, put into a small bowl and toss with the lemon juice to prevent browning.
6   Lift the pouch from the water bath and remove the brisket. Pat dry with kitchen paper and season.

7   Heat a little oil in a heavy-based frying pan until very hot, add the brisket and quickly sear until browned on all sides, or brush with a little oil and use a culinary blow torch. Put the meat on a board and use two forks to pull and shred the meat apart.

8   Warm the flour tortillas wraps. Scatter some of the spinach and rocket leaves over each wrap. Top with onion slices and some avocado. Pile the shredded beef down the centre and add a spoonful of soured cream and a dash of chilli sauce, if using. Tightly roll the wrap over the filling and cut in half to serve.

At the end of step 4, the vacuum-sealed food pouch can be ice-chilled and refrigerated for up to four days, or frozen.

Smoky Paprika Casserole

My version of the Hungarian classic goulash lends itself perfectly to cooking in the sous vide.

Serves: 4
Water bath cooking time: 12–14 hours

500g/1lb 2oz lean braising beef
1 tbsp vegetable oil
1 tsp ground smoked paprika
½ tsp ground nutmeg
To finish the dish
2 rindless streaky bacon rashers
2 onions
2 carrots
2 garlic cloves
1 green pepper
2 tbsp vegetable oil
300ml/½ pint beef stock
200g can tomatoes
2 tbsp tomato purée
1 tsp ground smoked paprika
½ tsp ground nutmeg
Salt and freshly milled black pepper
For the topping
1 garlic clove
8 thin slices toasted French bread
1 tbsp olive oil
1 tbsp tomato purée
5 tbsp grated cheese, such as Cheddar, Gouda or Red Leicester

1   Fill the water bath and preheat to 60°C/140°F.
2   Trim any fat from the beef and cut into bite-sized pieces. Heat a little oil in a pan until very hot. Add the beef and quickly sear the meat on all sides — you may need to do this in batches. Pat dry with kitchen paper. (If not using immediately, remove and drain the meat, ice and refrigerate until cold.)
3   Put the beef into a large pouch and add the ground smoked paprika and nutmeg. Massage the pouch to mix the meat and spices, push into a single, even layer and vacuum-seal.

4 When at temperature, put the pouch into the water bath, cover with the lid and cook for 12–14 hours.

5 To finish the dish, roughly chop the bacon rashers. Finely chop the onions, carrots and garlic cloves. Cut the pepper in half, remove and discard the seeds and stalk, then roughly chop.

6 Heat the oil in a large, heavy-based pan and fry the chopped bacon until golden brown, then remove with a slotted spoon and put to one side. Stir in the prepared onions, carrots, garlic and green pepper, cooking for a few minutes until these begin to soften.

7 Pour the stock and tomatoes into the pan and stir in the tomato purée, reserved bacon, paprika, nutmeg and a little seasoning. Bring just to the boil and cook for 25 minutes, stirring occasionally, until thick.

8 For the topping, cut the garlic clove in half and rub the cut surfaces over one side of all the toasted bread slices. Brush with a little oil and tomato purée and top with grated cheese. Place on a baking sheet and either put in a hot oven or under a hot grill until the cheese has melted and browned.

9 Lift the pouch from the water bath. Remove the meat and stir it into the hot bacon and tomato mix in the pan. Season to taste, then serve on wide plates with a lip and put two of the cheesy toasts on top of each plate. The bread will soak up the juices.

At the end of steps 3 or 4, the vacuum-sealed food pouch can be ice-chilled and refrigerated for up to four days, or frozen.

Sirloin Roast with a Nut Mustard Crust

A fine balance – a crust of walnuts and sage to complement the succulent sirloin roast.

Serves: 2
Water bath cooking time: 12–48 hours

1.3 kg/3lb boneless sirloin beef roasting joint
1 tsp freshly milled black pepper
1½ tsp ground sage
To finish the dish
200g/7oz walnut pieces
2 tbsp wholegrain mustard
1 tbsp vegetable oil
½ tsp ground sage
Salt and freshly milled black pepper
Your favourite vegetables, to serve

1   Fill the water bath and preheat to 60°C/140°F.
2   Trim the joint and pat dry with kitchen paper. Rub the black pepper and sage over the meat.
3   Put the beef joint into a large food pouch and vacuum-seal.
4   When at temperature, put the pouch into the water bath, cover with the lid and cook for 12–48 hours.
5   To finish the dish, heat the oven to 220°C/205°F fan/gas 7.
6   Finely chop and crush the walnuts. In a small bowl, mix together the walnuts, wholegrain mustard, oil and ground sage to form a paste. Season to taste with salt and pepper.
7   Lift the pouch from the water bath and remove the beef. Pat dry with kitchen paper and put into a roasting tin.
8   Spread the nutty paste over the beef. Put into the hot oven for about 6–8 minutes until the crust is golden. Alternatively use a culinary blow torch.
9   Remove the rib roast from the oven, carve into slices and serve with your favourite vegetables.

At the end of step 4, the vacuum-sealed food pouch can be ice-chilled and refrigerated for up to four days, or frozen.

Mustard and Pepper Steak with Beetroot Salad

Robust flavours in a classic and colourful combination.

Serves: 2
Water bath cooking time: 2.5cm/1in thick, 1–4 hours; 5cm/2in thick, 2–4 hours

2 sirloin steaks
1 tbsp wholegrain mustard
Few drops of pepper sauce
1 tsp vegetable oil
To finish the dish
2 carrots
2 small raw beetroot
150ml/¼ pint thick Greek yogurt
1 tbsp orange juice
3 spring onions
Salt and freshly milled black pepper
Oil, for frying
1 large handful of salad leaves, to serve

1 Fill the water bath and preheat to 60°C/140°F.
2 Trim the steaks and pat dry with kitchen paper. In a small bowl, mix together the wholegrain mustard, pepper sauce and vegetable oil.
3 Spread the mustard paste over both sides of the steaks, put into two food pouches and vacuum-seal.
4 When at temperature, put the pouches into the pouch rack and lower into the water bath, cover with the lid and cook for 1–4 hours (see timings above).
5 To finish the dish, scrub the carrots and beetroot and coarsely grate. Put them into a bowl and stir in the yogurt and orange juice. Thinly slice the spring onions and add to the beetroot salad. Season to taste.
6 Lift the pouches from the water bath and remove the steaks. Pat them dry with kitchen paper and season.
7 Heat a little oil in a heavy-based frying pan until very hot, add the steaks and quickly sear until browned on both sides, or brush with a little oil and use a culinary blow torch.
8 Serve the steak with the carrot and beetroot salad and salad leaves.

At the end of steps 3 or 4 the vacuum-sealed food pouches can be ice-chilled and refrigerated for up to four days, or frozen.

Herby Beef Burgers

Fun food with lots of variations. Try using different herbs in the burgers for a range of different flavours.

Serves: 2–4
Water bath cooking time: 2–4 hours

1 small red onion
500g/1lb 2oz good-quality minced beef
¼ tsp ground mixed herbs
Freshly milled black pepper
2 tbsp vegetable oil
To finish the dish
Salt, if needed
Oil, for frying
Burger buns, salad leaves, pickles and mayonnaise or tomato ketchup, to serve

1   Fill the water bath and preheat to 60°C/140°F.
2   Finely chop the onion. Put the minced beef into a bowl and thoroughly mix in the onion, mixed herbs and a little pepper.
3   To check if the amount of seasoning is to your liking, heat a little oil in a pan. Cook a teaspoon of the mixture and taste. Adjust the seasoning to taste.
4   With wet hands, shape the mixture into 8 balls and flatten each into a disc.
5   Put two burgers with a gap between them in each of four food pouches. Lightly vacuum-seal without over-pulsing so the burgers aren't crushed.
6   When at temperature, put the pouches into the pouch rack and lower into the water bath, cover with the lid and cook for 2–4 hours.
7   To finish the dish, lift the pouches from the water bath. Remove the burgers and dry on kitchen paper, seasoning with salt if needed.
8   Heat a little oil in a heavy-based frying pan until very hot, add the burgers and quickly sear until browned on both sides, or brush with a little oil and use a culinary blow torch.
9   Serve in burger buns with salad leaves, pickles and mayonnaise or tomato ketchup.

At the end of step 6, the vacuum-sealed food pouches can be ice-chilled and refrigerated for up to four days, or frozen.

4
Lamb

Lamb is a succulent and flavoursome meat. By using the sous vide you will discover how the water bath process helps to bring out those wonderful, moist, luscious flavours. I've used lots of aromatic herbs and spices in these recipes to complement the varied approaches to cooking with lamb. There's a distinctly Mediterranean influence, like the Lamb Steaks with Olive and Caper Topping (see page 72), the Moroccan Lamb (see page 64) with the multiple spice mix, ras-el-hanout, and the fragrant Shoulder Roast with Rosemary (see page 68). All seven of these lamb dishes will set your taste buds working to the full.

When cooking lamb sous vide remember to:
• Buy good-quality meat.
• Keep it chilled until ready to use.
• When putting meat into a sous vide pouch, fold back the top flap of the pouch. It's then easy to slide in the ingredients without them touching the outside of the pouch.
• Alcohol gives a metallic flavour to foods cooked sous vide. To avoid this, pour into a small pan and heat on the hob for a few minutes to drive off the alcohol.
• Salt can begin to cure the meat when longer cooking times are used, so I salt when the lamb comes out of the water bath.
• Joints, chops or ribs with a bone in them may puncture the pouch, so avoid over-pulsing. Wrap the ends of the bones in parchment paper.
• Liquids such as stock or wine may be drawn out of the pouch when vacuum-sealing, so don't over-pulse. I often freeze them in ice cube trays and drop a cube or two into the pouch instead.
• Unless otherwise indicated, the liquid in the pouch is discarded.
• Sear or brown lamb very quickly, as the lamb continues to cook once removed from the heat.
• Sous vide cooked lamb needs only a few minutes of resting time, rather than the longer time required with conventional cooking.

Lamb Shanks with Green Lentils

A rustic dish that's always popular, with this recipe you'll find the meat is so moist and tender it falls off the bone.

Serves: 4
Water bath cooking time: 12–48 hours

4 lamb shanks
3 tsp ground thyme
Freshly milled black pepper
To finish the dish
2 onions
2 garlic cloves
1 small bunch of fresh thyme
2 x 400g cans green lentils
Oil, for frying
300ml/½ pint lamb stock
1 bay leaf
Salt and freshly milled pepper

1   Fill the water bath and preheat to 60°C/140°F.
2   Trim the lamb shanks and pat dry with kitchen paper. Rub the ground thyme and some pepper all over them.
3   Wrap the bones with parchment paper, then put each shank into a food pouch. Vacuum-seal, being careful not to over-pulse otherwise the lamb bone may puncture the pouch.
4   When at temperature, put the pouches into the pouch rack and lower into the water bath, cover with the lid and cook for 12–48 hours.
5   To finish the dish, finely chop the onions and garlic cloves. Pull the thyme leaves from the stalks and finely chop. Drain the lentils.
6   Heat a little oil in a pan and cook the onions and garlic until softened and beginning to brown. Tip in the lentils, stock, bay leaf, chopped thyme and a little salt and pepper. Bring just to the boil, reduce the heat and cook for 15–18 minutes, stirring occasionally.

7　Lift the pouches from the water bath. Remove the shanks and dry on kitchen paper, then season, if needed.

8　Heat a little oil in a heavy-based frying pan until very hot, add the shanks and quickly sear until browned, or brush with a little oil and use a culinary blow torch.

9　Serve the lamb shanks on top of the lentil mix.

At the end of step 4, the vacuum-sealed food pouches can be ice-chilled and refrigerated for up to four days, or frozen.

Moroccan Lamb

An exotic-sounding dish in which the complex spice mix, ras-el-hanout, and the preserved lemons create a harmony of flavours.

Serves: 4
Water bath cooking time: 12–14 hours

500g/1lb 2oz lean lamb
2 tbsp vegetable oil
2 lemon slices
To finish the dish
2 onions
2 garlic cloves
6 ready-to-eat dried apricots
1 preserved lemon, or fresh lemon
1 small bunch of coriander
Oil, for frying
1 tbsp ras-el-hanout
425ml/¾ pint lamb stock
Salt and freshly milled black pepper
100g bag baby spinach leaves
Boiled rice, to serve

1   Trim any fat from the lamb and cut into bite-sized pieces.
2   Heat a little oil in a heavy-based pan until very hot. Add the lamb and quickly sear the meat on all sides — you may need to do this in batches. Pat dry with kitchen paper. (If not using immediately, remove and drain the meat, ice and refrigerate until cold.)
3   Fill the water bath and preheat to 60°C/140°F.
4   Put the lamb into two food pouches and add a tbsp of the oil and a lemon slice to each pouch. Push the ingredients into single, even layers and vacuum-seal.
5   When at temperature, put the pouches into the water bath, cover with the lid and cook for 12–14 hours.
6   To finish the dish, finely chop the onions and garlic and thinly slice the apricots. Cut the preserved lemon, if using, into thin strips, or grate the fresh lemon, cut it in half and squeeze out the juice. Chop the coriander.

7   Heat the oil in a large pan and cook the onions and garlic until softened and lightly browned. Add the apricots, preserved lemon or lemon rind and juice, ras-el-hanout spice, stock and seasoning. Bring just to the boil, then cook for 10 minutes. Stir in the spinach leaves and half the coriander. Cook for a further 5–8 minutes until everything is well blended.

8   Lift the pouches from the water bath. Remove the lamb and stir it into the hot sauce. Stir in the remaining coriander and serve with rice.

At the end of step 5, the vacuum-sealed food pouches can be ice-chilled and refrigerated for up to four days, or frozen.

Lamb Curry with Chickpeas

A very comforting curry. Chickpeas give substance to the dish, but you could try borlotti or pinto beans instead.

Serves: 4–6
Water bath cooking time: 12–24 hours

500g/1lb 2oz lean lamb
1 tbsp vegetable oil
1 tbsp curry powder
1 tsp ground cumin
Freshly milled black pepper
To finish the dish
2 medium onions
2 carrots
2 celery sticks
1 eating apple
1 tsp lemon juice
400g can chickpeas
Oil, for frying
1 tbsp curry powder or paste
½ tsp ground turmeric
300ml/½ pint lamb stock
400g can tomatoes
2 tbsp tomato purée
2 tbsp sultanas
Salt and freshly milled black pepper
Boiled rice, pickles, thick natural yogurt and poppadums, to serve

1   Fill the water bath and preheat to 60°C/140°F.
2   Trim any fat from the lamb and cut into bite-sized pieces.
3   Heat a little oil in a pan until very hot. Add the lamb and quickly sear the meat on all sides — you may need to do this in batches. Pat dry with kitchen paper. (If not using immediately, remove and drain the meat, ice and refrigerate until cold.)
4   Put the lamb into a large food pouch and add the curry powder, cumin and a little pepper. Massage the pouch to mix the meat and spices, push into a single, even layer and vacuum-seal. The pouch can be chilled in the fridge for 2 hours for the flavours to develop.

5   When at temperature, put the pouch into the water bath, cover
     with the lid and cook for 12–14 hours.
6   To finish the dish, finely chop the onions and carrots. Thinly
     slice the celery sticks. Peel, core and roughly chop the apple
     and sprinkle with the lemon juice to prevent browning. Drain
     the chickpeas.
7   Heat the oil in a large, heavy-based pan and fry the onions,
     carrots and celery until they begin to soften and brown. Stir in the
     curry paste or powder and turmeric and cook for 1 minute. Pour
     in the stock, tomatoes, tomato purée, chickpeas, apple, sultanas
     and a little seasoning. Bring just to the boil, then cook for 30
     minutes, stirring occasionally.
8   Lift the pouch from the water bath. Remove the lamb and stir into
     the curry mix in the pan. Season to taste.
10   Serve with rice, pickles, yogurt and poppadums.

At the end of step 5, the vacuum-sealed food pouches can be
ice-chilled and refrigerated for up to four days, or frozen.

Shoulder Roast with Rosemary

Rosemary is one of the classic combinations to cook with lamb and the fragrance of rosemary permeates this lovely dish.

Serves: 4–6
Water bath cooking time: 24–48 hours

800g/1lb 12oz boned shoulder of lamb
1 tsp dried rosemary
1 tbsp lemon zest
Freshly milled black pepper
To finish the dish
Salt and freshly milled black pepper
Oil, for frying
Mint jelly, to serve

1   Fill the water bath and preheat to 60°C/140°F.
2   Remove any string ties from the joint. Trim any excess fat from the lamb and cut a few shallow slits in the joint. Pat dry with kitchen paper. Rub the rosemary, lemon zest and some pepper over the lamb, pushing it into the slits.
3   Put the lamb into a large food pouch and vacuum-seal.
4   When at temperature, put the pouch into the water bath, cover with the lid and cook for 1–2 days.
5   To finish the dish, lift the pouch from the water bath and remove the lamb. Pat dry with kitchen paper and season.
6   Heat a little oil in a heavy-based frying pan until very hot, add the lamb and quickly sear until browned on all sides, or brush with a little oil and use a culinary blow torch. Put the meat on a board and carve into slices.
7   Serve with mint jelly.

At the end of step 4, the vacuum-sealed food pouch can be ice-chilled and refrigerated for up to four days, or frozen.

Rack of Lamb

Always very elegant on the plate, this looks particularly sophisticated dusted with pine nuts and sunflower seeds.

Serves: 2
Water bath cooking time: 12–48 hours

2 trimmed racks of lamb
Oil, for frying
1 tsp freshly milled black pepper
To finish the dish
2 tbsp pine nuts
2 tbsp sunflower seeds
Salt and freshly milled black pepper
Oil, for frying
Red currant jelly, to serve

1   Fill the water bath and preheat to 60°C/140°F.
2   Trim the racks of lamb and pat dry with kitchen paper. Heat a little oil in a pan until very hot. Add the racks and quickly sear the meat. Pat dry with kitchen paper and wrap the bones with parchment paper.
3   Put the racks of lamb into two food pouches with a little pepper and vacuum-seal, being careful not to over-pulse otherwise the bones may puncture the pouch.
4   When at temperature, put the pouches into the water bath, cover with the lid and cook for 12–48 hours.
5   To finish the dish, grind or process the pine nuts and sunflower seeds until quite fine. Tip into a bowl and add a little seasoning.
6   Lift the pouches from the water bath and remove the racks. Pat dry with kitchen paper and put them onto a baking sheet.
7   Brush with a little oil and press the nut and seed dust over the racks. Put under a hot grill for a few seconds to sear or brown the lamb. Alternatively use a culinary blow torch.
8   Serve with red currant jelly.

At the end of step 4, the vacuum-sealed food pouches can be ice-chilled and refrigerated for up to four days, or frozen.

Lamb Koftas

Cumin, coriander and cinnamon give lots of flavour to these spicy meatballs served with a cooling mint and yogurt dressing.

Serves: 4
Water bath cooking time: 2–4 hours

1 small red onion
500g/1lb 2oz lean minced lamb
1 tsp ground cumin
1 tsp ground coriander
Pinch of ground cinnamon
Freshly milled black pepper
2 tbsp vegetable oil
To finish the dish
1 small bunch of mint
300ml/½ pint thick Greek yogurt
Salt and freshly milled black pepper
Oil, for frying

1   Fill the water bath and preheat to 60°C/140°F.
2   Finely chop the onion. Put the minced lamb into a bowl and thoroughly mix in the onion, ground cumin, coriander, cinnamon and a little pepper.
3   To check if the amount of seasoning is to your liking, heat a little oil in a pan. Cook a teaspoon of the mixture and taste. Adjust the seasoning to taste. If there's time, cover the mixture and chill for 2 hours for the flavours to develop.
4   With wet hands, shape the mixture into 12 balls.
5   Arrange the koftas, with gaps between them, in four food pouches. Lightly vacuum-seal without over-pulsing so the koftas aren't crushed.
6   When at temperature, put the pouches into the pouch rack and lower into the water bath, cover with the lid and cook for 2–4 hours.

7 To finish the dish, pull the mint leaves from the stalks and finely chop. Pour the yogurt into a bowl and stir in the mint and plenty of seasoning. Chill until needed.

8 Lift the pouches from the water bath. Remove the koftas and dry on kitchen paper. Season with salt if needed.

9 Heat a little oil in a heavy-based frying pan until very hot, add the koftas and quickly sear until browned all over, or brush with a little oil and use a culinary blow torch.

10 Serve with the mint and yogurt dressing.

At the end of step 6, the vacuum-sealed food pouches can be ice-chilled and refrigerated for up to four days, or frozen.

Lamb Steaks with Olive and Caper Topping

One of my favourite crunchy topping mixes for almost any savoury dish is capers, olives, garlic and a few sourdough crumbs. It's always useful to have a jar of capers handy.

Serves: 2
Water bath cooking time: 2.5cm/1in thick, 1–4 hours; 5cm/2in thick, 2–4 hours

2 x 175g/6oz lamb leg steaks on the bone
Freshly milled black pepper
To finish the dish
1 tbsp capers in brine
1 garlic clove
8 stoned green olives
Oil, for frying
1 large handful of sourdough breadcrumbs
Salt and freshly milled black pepper

1   Fill the water bath and preheat to 60°C/140°F.
2   Trim the steaks and pat dry with kitchen paper.
3   Put the steaks into two food pouches and add a little pepper to each pouch. Vacuum-seal, being careful not to over-pulse otherwise the lamb bone may puncture the pouch.
4   When at temperature, put the pouches into the pouch rack and lower into the water bath, cover with the lid and cook for 1–4 hours (see timings above).
5   To finish the dish, rinse and drain the capers, then cut them in half. Crush the garlic and slice the olives.
6   Heat a little oil in a frying pan. Stir in the breadcrumbs and garlic and cook until they begin to brown. Tip in the capers and olives and heat through. Season to taste.
7   Lift the pouches from the water bath and remove the steaks. Pat them dry with kitchen paper and season.
8   Heat a little oil in a heavy-based frying pan until very hot, add the steaks and quickly sear until browned on both sides, or brush with a little oil and use a culinary blow torch. Spoon the olive crumbs onto each steak and serve immediately.

At the end of step 4, the vacuum-sealed food pouches can be ice-chilled and refrigerated for up to four days, or frozen.

5
Pork

Juicy, mellow pork has long been a firm favourite, and with good reason. You'll be delighted by the way your sous vide handles both traditional and fashionable styles of cooking pork with equal ease. Tempting versions of classic pork dishes can be found in this chapter, including Chump Chops with Cider and Apples (see page 84) and a Slow-cooked Spicy Pork joint (see page 74), infused with spices and served with that classic pork accompaniment, apple sauce. Here, too, are recipes for the ever-popular Barbecue-style Sticky Spare Ribs (see page 82), a subtle, spicy Oriental Pork Stir-fry (see page 76) to go with hot rice or noodles, and a Sticky Jerk Pork (see page 83), all guaranteed to have wide appeal.

When cooking pork sous vide remember to:
- Buy good-quality meat.
- Keep it chilled until ready to use.
- When putting meat into a sous vide pouch, fold back the top flap of the pouch. It's then easy to slide in the ingredients without them touching the outside of the pouch.
- Alcohol gives a metallic flavour to foods cooked sous vide. To avoid this, pour into a small pan and heat on the hob for a few minutes to drive off the alcohol.
- Salt can begin to cure the meat when longer cooking times are used, so I salt when the meat comes out of the water bath.
- Joints, chops or ribs with a bone in them may puncture the pouch, so avoid over-pulsing. Wrap the ends of the bones in parchment paper.
- Liquids such as stock or wine may be drawn out of the pouch when vacuum-sealing, so don't over-pulse. I often freeze them in ice cube trays and drop a cube or two into the pouch instead.
- Sear or brown meat very quickly, as the meat continues to cook during this process.
- Sous vide cooked pork needs only a few minutes resting time rather than the longer time required with conventional cooking.

Slow-cooked Spicy Pork

The meat is rubbed with a spice mix of cloves, cinnamon and pepper, plus a little sage. Sage can over-power a dish, so it is better to use a small quantity, whether fresh, dried or ground.

Serves: 4–6
Water bath cooking time: 24–72 hours

Water bath ingredients
2 tsp ground cloves
2 tsp ground cinnamon
2 tsp freshly milled black pepper
Good pinch of ground sage
1.35 kg/3lb 5oz boneless pork leg joint
To finish the dish
Oil, for frying
Roasted vegetables and apple sauce, to serve

1   Fill the water bath and preheat to 60°C/140°F.
2   In a small bowl, mix together the ground cloves, cinnamon, pepper and sage. Remove any ties from the pork. Trim and pat dry with kitchen paper. Sprinkle three teaspoons of the spice mix over the pork and rub all over the meat. Reserve the remaining spice mix to use later in the recipe.
3   Put the pork joint into a large food pouch and vacuum-seal.
4   When at temperature, put the food pouch into the water bath, cover with the lid and cook for 1-3 days.

5   To finish the dish, lift the pouch from the water bath and remove the pork. Pat dry with kitchen paper. Rub the remaining spice mix over the pork joint.
6   Heat a little oil in a heavy-based frying pan until very hot, add the pork and quickly sear until browned on all sides, or alternatively brush with a little oil and use a culinary blow torch.
7   Put the meat on a board and carve into slices. Serve with roasted vegetables and apple sauce.

At the end of step 4, the vacuum-sealed food pouch can be ice-chilled and refrigerated for up to four days, or frozen.

Oriental Pork Stir-fry

For a light, fresh stir-fry, always have your ingredients to hand so you can finish the dish quickly and serve it at its best.

Serves: 4
Water bath cooking time: 10-14 hours

500g/1lb 2oz lean pork
Oil, for frying
¼ tsp chilli powder
Freshly milled black pepper
2 lemon slices
To finish the dish
6 spring onions
6 small chestnut mushrooms
Small piece of root ginger
1 red pepper
2 handfuls of pak choi or spinach leaves
2 tbsp vegetable oil
150ml/¼ pint vegetable stock
1 tbsp light soy sauce
2 tbsp sweet chilli sauce
Salt and freshly milled black pepper
1 tbsp toasted sesame seeds
Hot rice or noodles, to serve

1   Fill the water bath and preheat to 60°C/140°F.
2   Trim any fat from the pork and cut into bite-sized pieces.
3   Heat a little oil in a heavy-based pan until very hot. Add the pork and quickly sear the meat on all sides — you may need to do this in batches. Pat dry with kitchen paper. (If not using immediately, remove and drain the meat, ice and refrigerate until cold.)
4   Put the pork into a large food pouch, adding the chilli powder and a little black pepper. Massage the pouch to mix the ingredients and drop the lemon slices into the pouch. Push into a single, even layer and vacuum-seal.

5   When at temperature, put the pouch nto the water bath, cover with the lid and cook for 10–14 hours.

6   To finish the dish, thinly slice the spring onions and mushrooms. Grate the root ginger. Halve the red pepper, remove and discard the seeds and stalk, and slice thinly. Tear the pak choi or spinach leaves if they are large.

7   Heat a wok or large pan and add the oil, spring onions and ginger, cooking for a few seconds. Then add the mushrooms and red pepper and cook for a few minutes until lightly browned. Add the pak choi or spinach leaves, stock, soy sauce, chilli sauce and seasoning. Bring just to the boil and cook for a few minutes.

8   Lift the pouch from the water bath. Remove the pork and add it to the stir fry. Gently mix together and season to taste. Sprinkle over the sesame seeds and serve with hot rice or noodles.

At the end of step 5, the vacuum-sealed food pouches can be ice-chilled and refrigerated for up to four days, or frozen.

Bacon-wrapped Pork Tenderloin with Lemon and Parsley

Hidden in the middle, a little zesty mix will surprise you with a burst of flavour from the inside.

Serves: 4–6
Water bath cooking time: 8-12 hours

1 handful of parsley leaves
1 tbsp lemon zest
Freshly milled black pepper
550g/1lb 4oz pork tenderloin in two pieces
4 thin rindless smoked streaky bacon rashers
To finish the dish
Oil, for frying
Salt and freshly milled black pepper
Couscous and mange tout, to serve

1   Fill the water bath and preheat to 60°C/140°F.
2   Finely chop the parsley and put this into a small pan. Stir in the lemon zest and pepper to taste. Add a tablespoon of water. Bring just to boiling point until the water is driven off and the parsley and lemon zest are cooked. Put into a little dish and chill until cold.
3   Pat dry the two pieces of pork with kitchen paper. Cut a slit along the length of each, without cutting all the way through, and open out the pork.
4   Thinly spread the parsley and lemon mix along the middle of both pieces of pork. Fold the pork over the filling and wrap the bacon around the two pieces of pork.
5   Put the stuffed and wrapped pork into two food pouches and vacuum-seal.

6   When at temperature, put the pouches into the water bath, cover with the lid and cook for 8–12 hours.

7   To finish the dish, lift the pouches from the water bath and remove the pork. Pat dry with kitchen paper.

8   Heat a little oil in a heavy-based frying pan until very hot. Quickly turn the pork in the pan for a few seconds to brown and crisp the meat. Alternatively use a culinary blow torch. Season to taste.

9   Carve into thick slices and serve with couscous and mange tout.

At the end of step 6, the vacuum-sealed food pouches can be ice-chilled and refrigerated for up to four days, or frozen.

Sweet and Sour Pork

This is my variation on a well-liked dish. In the sous vide, the meat is always reliably tender.

Serves: 4
Water bath cooking time: 12–14 hours

500g/1lb 2oz lean pork
Oil, for frying
Freshly milled black pepper
To finish the dish
1 onion
1 garlic clove
1 red chilli
Small piece of root ginger
Oil, for frying
300ml/½ pint vegetable or chicken stock
200g can crushed pineapple
1 tbsp light soy sauce
1 tbsp sugar
1 tbsp white wine vinegar
Pinch of ground star anise
1 tbsp cornflour (optional)
Salt and freshly milled black pepper
Rice, noodles or polenta, to serve

1   Fill the water bath and preheat to 60°C/140°F.
2   Trim any fat from the pork and cut into bite-sized pieces.
3   Heat a little oil in a heavy-based pan until very hot. Add the pork and quickly sear the meat on all sides — you may need to do this in batches. Pat dry with kitchen paper. (If not using immediately, remove and drain the meat, ice and refrigerate until cold.)
4   Put the pork into a large food pouch and add a little pepper. Push into a single, even layer and vacuum-seal.
5   When at temperature, put the pouch into the water bath, cover with the lid and cook for 12–14 hours.

6   To finish the dish, finely chop the onion and garlic. Cut the chilli in half, remove and discard the stalk and seeds, then slice very finely. Grate the ginger.

7   Heat the oil in a large, heavy-based pan and fry the onion, garlic and chilli until softened. Pour in the stock and the can of pineapple, including the juice. Stir in the ginger, soy sauce, sugar, vinegar and star anise. Bring just to the boil, then cook for 20 minutes, stirring occasionally. If you prefer a thicker sauce, mix the cornflour in a cup with a little cold water until smooth. Stir into the sauce and cook until thickened, stirring continuously.

8   Lift the pouch from the water bath. Remove the pork and stir into the sweet and sour mix. Season to taste and serve with rice, noodles or polenta.

At the end of step 5, the vacuum-sealed food pouch can be ice-chilled and refrigerated for up to four days, or frozen.

Barbecue-style Sticky Spare Ribs

Rich and more-ish with bags of flavour – have your paper napkins at the ready.

Serves: 4
Water bath cooking time: 12–48 hours

900g/2lb lean pork spare ribs
1 tsp smoked paprika
1 tsp freshly milled black pepper
¼ tsp mustard powder
To finish the dish
1 tbsp soft brown sugar
4 tbsp tomato ketchup
2 tbsp Worcestershire sauce
½ tsp smoked paprika
¼ tsp mustard powder
Salt and freshly milled black pepper

1   Fill the water bath and preheat to 60°C/140°F.
2   Trim the spare ribs and cut into individual portions. Pat dry with kitchen paper. Mix the paprika, black pepper and mustard powder together in a small bowl. Rub the spices all over the ribs. Wrap any sharp bones with parchment paper.
3   Arrange the ribs into in a single layer in each of four food pouches. Vacuum-seal, being careful not to over-pulse otherwise the bones may puncture the pouches.
4   When at temperature, put the pouches into the pouch holder and lower into the water bath, cover with the lid and cook for 12–48 hours.
5   To finish the dish, heat the oven to 220°C/205°F fan/Gas 7.
6   Pour 5 tbsp of water into a pan and stir in the sugar, ketchup, Worcestershire sauce, paprika and mustard powder. Bring to the boil, then simmer for 15 minutes.
7   Lift the pouches from the water bath and remove the ribs. Pat dry with kitchen paper and arrange in a single layer on a shallow roasting tin.
8   Drizzle or brush the sauce over the ribs, making sure they are covered. Cook in the hot oven for about 5 minutes until beginning to brown. Drizzle over any remaining sauce and quickly cook until browned. Alternatively use a culinary blow torch. Season to taste.

At the end of step 4, the vacuum-sealed food pouches can be ice-chilled and refrigerated for up to four days, or frozen.

Sticky Jerk Pork

This is packed with sunshine and Jamaican flavouring, so it's nice and lively.

Serves: 4–6
Water bath cooking time: 48–72 hours

650g/1lb 7oz boned and rolled pork roasting joint
1 tsp jerk seasoning
Freshly milled black pepper
To finish the dish
½ tsp jerk seasoning
2 tbsp unsweetened pineapple juice
2 tsp oil
1 tbsp soft brown sugar
Salt and freshly milled black pepper
Jacket potatoes and salad, to serve

1   Fill the water bath and preheat to 60°C/140°F.
2   Remove any string ties from the pork, unroll and flatten out. With
    a sharp knife, score criss-cross lines through the fat. Pat dry with
    kitchen paper and rub the jerk seasoning and a little pepper all
    over the pork.
3   Put the seasoned joint into a large food pouch and vacuum-seal.
4   When at temperature, put the pouch into the water bath, cover
    with the lid and cook for 48–72 hours.
5   To finish the dish, in a small pan mix together the jerk seasoning,
    pineapple juice, oil, brown sugar and a little salt and pepper.
    Gently heat, stirring constantly, until the sugar has dissolved.
6   Lift the pouch from the water bath and remove the pork. Pat dry
    with kitchen paper. Put the pork onto a baking tray and spread
    the sticky topping over the top of the pork. Put the pork under a
    very hot grill for seconds to brown the topping, making sure it
    doesn't burn, or use a culinary blow torch or hot oven.
7   Put the meat on a board and use two forks to pull and shred the
    meat apart. Serve with jacket potatoes and salad.

At the end of step 4, the vacuum-sealed food pouch can be ice-
chilled and refrigerated for up to four days, or frozen.

Chump Chops with Cider and Apples

Chump chops are a very meaty traditional pork cut, so this makes a generous meal, which is lovely served with mashed potatoes and seasonal vegetables.

Serves: 2–4
Water bath cooking time: 4–8 hours

4 pork chump chops
Freshly milled black pepper
To finish the dish
2 medium onions
2 eating apples
Oil, for frying
5 tbsp dry cider
150ml/¼ pint chicken stock
Pinch of ground cinnamon
Salt and freshly milled black pepper
Oil, for frying

1   Fill the water bath and preheat to 60°C/140°F.
2   Trim the chops and pat dry with kitchen paper. Put each chop into a 'food pouch and add a little pepper. Wrap the bones in parchment paper.
3   Vacuum-seal, being careful not to over-pulse otherwise the bone may puncture the pouch.
4   When at temperature, put the pouches into the pouch rack and lower into the water bath, cover with the lid and cook for 4–8 hours.
5   To finish, finely chop the onions. Peel, core and chop the apples.
6   Heat a little oil in a pan and cook the onions until softened and starting to brown. Add the apples, cider, stock, cinnamon and a little seasoning. Bring to the boil, then cook for 15 minutes until the onion and apple are soft. Use a stick blender or a processor to purée until smooth. Season to taste.
7   Lift the pouches from the water bath and remove the chops. Pat them dry with kitchen paper and season.
8   Heat a little oil in a heavy-based frying pan until very hot, add the chops and quickly sear until browned on both sides, or brush with a little oil and use a culinary blow torch.
9   Serve the chops with the apple cider purée poured over them.

At the end of step 4, the vacuum-sealed food pouches can be ice-chilled and refrigerated for up to four days, or frozen.

6
Poultry

Chicken is a real mainstay of the kitchen, being both economical and adaptable. It's also highly nutritious. See what stunning results can be achieved by sampling the chicken recipes in this chapter – such as Chicken with Lime and Peanuts (see page 86) and Chicken and Chorizo (see page 88) – all of them delivering bags of flavour and great for any day of the week or that special treat. For chicken with a difference, look out for distinctive breeds like mild, gamey-flavoured poulet noir, a popular French variety, or corn-fed chicken with its golden-coloured flesh. For poultry with a difference, there are two enticing turkey dishes and a succulent duck breast with plum salsa. And finally, to show off another successful side to your trusty sous vide, try Scrambled Eggs with Smoked Salmon (see page 100) or Eggs and Buttered Asparagus (see page 99) for breakfast or brunch.

When cooking poultry sous vide remember to:
- Buy good-quality poultry.
- Keep it chilled until ready to use.
- When putting poultry into a sous vide pouch, fold back the top flap of the pouch. It's then easy to slide in the ingredients without them touching the outside of the pouch.
- Alcohol gives a metallic flavour to foods cooked sous vide, so pour into a small pan and heat on the hob for a few minutes to drive off the alcohol.
- Salt can begin to cure the poultry when longer cooking times are used, so I salt when the game comes out of the water bath.
- Portions such as legs, thighs or breast on the bone may puncture the pouch, so avoid over-pulsing. Wrap the ends of the bones in parchment paper.
- Liquids such as stock or wine may be drawn out of the pouch when vacuum-sealing, so don't over-pulse. I often freeze them in ice cube trays and drop a cube or two into the pouch instead.
- Unless otherwise indicated, the liquid in the pouch is discarded.
- Sear or brown poultry very quickly, as the poultry continues to cook when removed from the heat.
- Sous vide cooked poultry needs only a few minutes resting time, rather than the longer time required with conventional cooking.

Chicken with Lime and Peanuts

There's a Far-Eastern feel to this dish, which works equally well with turkey.

Serves: 4
Water bath cooking time: 2–3 hours

4 boneless, skinless chicken breasts
2 tbsp oil
Freshly milled pepper
To finish the dish
1 small onion
1 garlic clove
1 lime
1 Chinese leaves lettuce
2 carrots
Oil, for frying
300ml/½ pint chicken stock
Salt and freshly milled black pepper
3 tbsp crunchy peanut butter
2 tbsp light soy sauce

1   Fill the water bath and preheat to 60°C/140°F.
2   Pat dry the chicken breasts with kitchen paper and put each into a food pouch. Add some oil and a little pepper to each one and vacuum-seal.
3   When at temperature, put the pouches into the pouch rack and lower into the water bath, cover with the lid and cook for 2–3 hours.
4   To finish the dish, finely chop the onion and garlic. Grate the zest from the lime, cut in half and squeeze out the juice. Finely shred the Chinese leaves. Cut the carrots into matchstick-sized pieces.
5   Heat a little oil in a pan and cook the onion and garlic until softened and beginning to brown. Add the stock, lime zest and juice, Chinese leaves, carrots and a little seasoning. Bring just to the boil, then reduce the heat and cook for 15 minutes, stirring occasionally. Stir in the peanut butter and soy sauce, then cook for a further 5 minutes. Season to taste.

6   Lift the pouches from the water bath. Remove the chicken breasts and dry on kitchen paper, seasoning if needed.

7   Heat a little oil in a heavy-based frying pan until very hot, add the chicken breasts and quickly sear until browned on one side, or brush with a little oil and use a culinary blow torch.

8   Slice each chicken breast into four and serve in wide bowls with the vegetables spooned over.

At the end of step 3, the vacuum-sealed food pouches can be ice-chilled and refrigerated for up to four days, or frozen.

Chicken and Chorizo

Chorizo is a highly seasoned sausage used in Spanish cookery. It really adds a bit of a punch.

Serves: 4
Water bath cooking time: 6 –10 hours

500g/1lb 2oz chicken
2 tbsp vegetable oil
To finish the dish
1 onion
150g/5½oz chorizo
Oil, for frying
150ml/¼ pint chicken stock
200g can tomatoes
200g/7oz sweetcorn
Salt and freshly milled black pepper

1 Fill the water bath and preheat to 60°C/140°F.
2 Cut the chicken into bite-sized pieces.
3 Put the chicken into two food pouches and add a little oil to each pouch. Push into single, even layers and vacuum-seal.
4 When at temperature, put the pouches into the water bath, cover with the lid and cook for 6–10 hours.
5 To finish, finely chop the onion. Slice the chorizo sausage.
6 Heat some oil in a large pan and cook the chorizo and onion until browned. Stir in the stock, tomatoes, sweetcorn and seasoning. Bring just to the boil, then cook for 20 minutes.
7 Lift the pouches from the water bath. Remove the chicken and pat dry on kitchen paper.
8 In a separate pan, heat a little oil until very hot, add the chicken and quickly sear until browned all over. Drain the chicken and stir into the chorizo mix. Season to taste and serve.

At the end of step 4, the vacuum-sealed food pouches can be ice-chilled and refrigerated for up to four days, or frozen.

Sticky Chicken Drumsticks

Get stuck in!

Serves: 4
Water bath cooking time: 8–14 hours

8 chicken drumsticks
½ tsp smoked paprika
1 tsp freshly milled black pepper
To finish the dish
2–3 tbsp golden syrup
4 tbsp tomato ketchup
Salt and freshly milled black pepper

1   Fill the water bath and preheat to 60°C/140°F.
2   Trim the drumsticks and pat dry with kitchen paper. Make two or three shallow cuts on each drumstick, then rub the paprika and black pepper all over. Wrap any sharp bones with parchment paper.
3   Put two drumsticks in each of four food pouches, keeping the drumsticks separate (see note on page 46), and vacuum-seal.
4   When at temperature, put the pouches into the pouch holder and lower into the water bath, cover with the lid and cook for 8–14 hours.
5   To finish the dish, in a bowl mix together the golden syrup and tomato ketchup.
6   Lift the pouches from the water bath and remove the drumsticks. Pat dry with kitchen paper and arrange in a single layer on a shallow roasting tin. Drizzle or brush the sauce over the drumsticks. Put under a hot grill and turn the drumsticks to quickly brown them all over. Alternatively use a culinary blow torch. Season to taste.

At the end of step 4, the vacuum-sealed food pouches can be ice-chilled and refrigerated for up to four days, or frozen.

Mild Curried Chicken

A chicken leg portion with a lightly spiced onion sauce, perfect for mid-week.

Serves: 2
Water bath cooking time: 12–48 hours

2 chicken leg portions
2 tsp curry powder
2 tbsp oil
To finish the dish
2 red onions
1 large handful of parsley leaves
Oil, for frying
2 tbsp mild curry paste
300ml/½ pint chicken stock
Salt and freshly milled black pepper

1   Fill the water bath and preheat to 60°C/140°F.
2   Trim the chicken portions and make two or three cuts through the flesh on each piece. Pat dry with kitchen paper. Rub the curry powder all over the chicken and wrap any sharp bones with parchment paper.
3   Put the chicken portions into two food pouches, adding a little of the oil to moisten. Vacuum-seal, being careful not to over-pulse, otherwise the bones may puncture the pouches.
4   When at temperature, put the pouches into the water bath, cover with the lid and cook for 12–48 hours.
5   To finish the dish, finely chop the onions. Roughly chop the parsley.
6   Heat some oil in a pan and cook the onions until softened and browned. Stir in the curry paste, stock, parsley and a little seasoning. Bring just to the boil, then cook for 30 minutes until the onions are very soft.
7   Lift the pouches from the water bath and remove the chicken portions. Pat dry with kitchen paper.
8   Heat a little oil in a heavy-based frying pan until very hot, add the chicken and quickly sear until browned on both sides, or brush with a little oil and use a culinary blow torch.
9   Serve the chicken portions with the onion sauce spooned over.

At the end of step 4, the vacuum-sealed food pouches can be ice-chilled and refrigerated for up to four days, or frozen.

Chicken Fritters

I like to put these tasty treats into warm pitta breads with some crisp, fresh salad.

Serves: up to 8
Water bath cooking time: 2–4 hours

1 small onion
350g/12oz minced chicken
1 tsp lemon zest
2 tbsp chopped parsley
Freshly milled black pepper
Oil, for frying
To finish the dish
Salt and freshly milled black pepper
Oil, for frying
Warmed pitta breads
Salad leaves
Sweet chilli sauce
Thick natural yogurt

1   Fill the water bath and preheat to 60°C/140°F.
2   Finely chop the onion. Put the minced chicken into a bowl and thoroughly mix in the onion, lemon zest, parsley and a little pepper.
3   To check if the amount of seasoning is to your liking, heat a little oil in a pan. Cook a teaspoon of the mixture and taste. Adjust the seasoning to taste.
4   With wet hands, shape the mixture into 8 balls and flatten.
5   Arrange the fritters, with gaps between them, in four food pouches. Use a light vacuum-seal without over-pulsing so the fritters aren't crushed.
6   When at temperature, put the pouches into the pouch rack and lower into the water bath, cover with the lid and cook for 2–4 hours.
7   To finish the dish, lift the pouches from the water bath. Remove the fritters and dry on kitchen paper, then season to taste.
8   Heat a little oil in a heavy-based frying pan until very hot, add the fritters and quickly sear until browned all over, or brush with a little oil and use a culinary blow torch.
9   Cut the warm pitta breads open and put a chicken fritter into each one. Top with salad leaves, a blob of chilli sauce and a spoonful of yogurt.

Hot Turkey Bagels

Kids will love these deconstructed bagels.

Serves: 4–6
Water bath cooking time: 12–14 hours

350g/12oz thick slice boneless turkey breast
1 tsp allspice
Freshly milled black pepper
1 tbsp oil
To finish the dish
1 red onion
Tomatoes
Gherkins
Salt and freshly milled black pepper
Oil, for frying
Hot bagels
Wholegrain mustard
Salad leaves
Mayonnaise
Cranberry sauce

1   Fill the water bath and preheat to 60°C/140°F.
2   Pat dry the turkey breast with kitchen paper and rub the allspice and some pepper all over the meat.
3   Put the turkey into a large pouch. Add the oil and vacuum-seal.
4   When at temperature, put the pouch into the water bath, cover with the lid and cook for 12–14 hours.
5   To finish the dish, thinly slice the onion, tomatoes and gherkins. Lift the pouch from the water bath and remove the meat. Pat dry with kitchen paper and season.

6   Heat a little oil in a heavy-based frying pan until very hot, add the turkey and quickly sear until browned on both sides, or brush with a little oil and use a culinary blow torch. Put the meat on a board and use two forks to pull and shred the meat apart.

7   Warm the bagels. Put all the ingredients on separate plates and let people build up their own filled bagels.

At the end of step 4, the vacuum-sealed food pouch can be ice-chilled and refrigerated for up to four days, or frozen.

Turkey with Creamy Bacon and Tarragon Sauce

A touch of refinement is brought to this dish by the tarragon.

Serves: 2
Water bath cooking time: 2–4 hours

350g/12oz slice boneless turkey breast
2 tbsp oil
½ tsp dried tarragon
Freshly milled pepper
To finish the dish
1 shallot
1 garlic clove
2 rashers smoked back bacon
1 sprig of tarragon
Oil, for frying
100ml/3½fl oz dry white wine or unsweetened white grape juice
300ml/½ pint chicken stock
Salt and freshly milled pepper
125ml/4fl oz double cream

1   Fill the water bath and preheat to 60°C/140°F.
2   Cut the turkey into bite-sized pieces and pat dry with kitchen paper.
3   Put the meat into two food pouches. Add a little oil, dried tarragon and a little pepper to each pouch, then vacuum-seal.
4   When at temperature, put the pouches into the pouch rack and lower into the water bath, cover with the lid and cook for 2–4 hours.
5   To finish the dish, finely chop the shallot and garlic. Remove and discard any rinds from the bacon rashers and finely chop the meat. Pull the leaves from the tarragon and chop finely.
6   Heat a little oil in a pan and cook the bacon, shallot and garlic until softened and beginning to brown. Add the wine or grape juice, stock, a little seasoning and half of the tarragon.

7   Bring just to the boil, then reduce the heat and cook for 10 minutes. Pour in the cream and cook for 10 minutes, stirring occasionally. Season to taste.

8   Lift the pouches from the water bath. Remove the turkey meat and dry on kitchen paper. Season if needed.

9   Heat a little oil in a heavy-based frying pan until very hot, add the turkey and quickly sear until browned on each side, or brush with a little oil and use a culinary blow torch.

10 Drain the turkey and stir into the creamy bacon sauce. Serve immediately.

At the end of step 4, the vacuum-sealed food pouches can be ice-chilled and refrigerated for up to four days, or frozen.

Duck with Plum Salsa

Cooking this dish in the sous vide machine makes for succulent duck, which I serve with a piquant salsa.

Serves: 2
Water bath cooking time: 4–6 hours

2 duck breasts
Freshly milled black pepper
For the salsa
200g/7oz ripe plums
1 small shallot
2.5cm/1in piece of fresh root ginger
1 tbsp clear honey
To finish the dish
1 red onion
1 small fennel bulb
Oil, for frying
2 tbsp chicken stock
1 tbsp grated orange zest
2 tsp cider vinegar
1 tsp clear honey
Salt and freshly milled black pepper

1   Fill the water bath and preheat to 60°C/140°F.
2   Cut criss-cross lines through the skin and fat on the duck breasts and pat dry with kitchen paper.
3   Put the meat into two food pouches and add a little pepper to each pouch. Vacuum-seal.
4   When at temperature, put the pouches into the pouch rack and lower into the water bath, cover with the lid and cook for 4–6 hours.
5   To finish the dish, make the salsa. Halve the plums, remove the stones and chop finely. Grate the shallot and ginger. Spoon the honey into a bowl and stir in the plums, shallot and ginger. Season to taste, then chill until needed.
6   Very thinly slice the onion and fennel bulb.

7   Heat a little oil in a heavy-based frying pan and cook the onion and fennel until lightly browned and cooked through. Lift out the cooked vegetables and wipe out the pan with kitchen paper. Reheat the pan and add the stock, orange zest, vinegar and honey. Heat until bubbling, then gently stir in the vegetables until coated in the sauce. Season to taste.

8   Lift the pouches from the water bath and remove the duck breasts. Pat them dry with kitchen paper and season.

9   Heat a little oil in a heavy-based frying pan until very hot, add the meat fat-side down and quickly sear until the fat has browned, or use a culinary blow torch.

10 Cut each duck breast into thick slices and serve on top of a pile of the vegetables. Offer the salsa alongside.

At the end of step 4, the vacuum-sealed food pouches can be ice-chilled and refrigerated for up to four days, or frozen.

Eggs

When you cook eggs in the sous vide, they are cooked in their shells and should not be vacuum-sealed. Twelve hens' eggs can be cooked at a time. Using a slotted spoon, put them on the grill in the bottom of the water bath and let them cook.

Fast soft-cooked large hen's egg: 75°C/167°F for 15–18 minutes
Slow soft-cooked large hen's egg: 63.5°C/146°F for 45–90 minutes
Hard-cooked large hen's egg: 71°C/160°F for 45–90 minutes

Eggs and Buttered Asparagus

A breakfast or brunch speciality, buy asparagus in season for the best flavour.

Serves: 2
Water bath cooking time: 15–18 minutes

2 large hens' eggs
To finish the dish
12 asparagus spears
4 tbsp unsalted butter
Salt and freshly milled black pepper

1 Fill the water bath and preheat to 75°C/167°F.
2 When at temperature, put the eggs into the water bath, cover with the lid and cook for 45–90 minutes.
3 To finish the dish, bend and snap the woody ends off the asparagus spears. Scrape or peel the end of the spears.
4 Heat the butter in a large, ridged frying pan. Cook the asparagus until tender. Put the asparagus onto plates, season and spoon over the remaining hot butter.
5 With a slotted spoon, lift the eggs from the water bath. Crack the eggs and scoop the soft egg on top of the hot asparagus. Season to taste.

Scrambled Eggs with Smoked Salmon

A classic combination, this must be high on everyone's Sunday brunch list, and the dish cooks beautifully using the sous vide method.

Serves: 2
Water bath cooking time: 20 minutes

5 large hens' eggs
Salt and freshly milled black pepper
1 tsp unsalted butter, softened
To finish the dish
1 lemon
4 slices oak-smoked salmon
Chopped chervil
Slices of brown bread and butter, to serve

1 Fill the water bath and preheat to 75°C/167°F.
2 Break the eggs into a bowl and add a little seasoning. With a fork, whisk until thoroughly mixed. Add 1 tsp of unsalted butter.
3 Pour the egg mixture into a food pouch. Press out the air and seal. Do not vacuum-seal.
4 When at temperature, put the pouch into the water bath, cover with the lid and cook for 20 minutes. Every few minutes, take the pouch out of the water bath and agitate or massage to move the mixture around.
5 To finish the dish, cut the lemon into wedges. Fold the salmon onto plates. Spoon the scrambled eggs on top. Sprinkle over the chervil, and serve with lemon wedges and slices of brown bread and butter.

7
Game

Game may not be the first thing that comes to mind when you think of cooking sous vide, but it's definitely worth a try. It's natural to think of meat hung for weeks acquiring pronounced and intense flavours, but depending on how it's reared and handled, game can also be quite delicate. It's always a lean meat, so a good healthy option. Tantalizing recipes in this chapter using venison, rabbit, pheasant or mixed packs of game show how your sous vide can help you serve up some really vibrant and exciting meals. Not to be missed, there's a good choice of game to be had in the shops all year round.

When cooking game sous vide remember to:
• Buy good-quality game.
• Keep it chilled until ready to use.
• When putting game into a sous vide pouch, fold back the top flap of the pouch. It's then easy to slide in the ingredients without them touching the outside of the pouch.
• Alcohol gives a metallic flavour to foods cooked sous vide. To avoid this, pour into a small pan and heat on the hob for a few minutes to drive off the alcohol.
• Salt can begin to cure the game when longer cooking times are used, so I salt when the game comes out of the water bath.
• Joints, chops or ribs with a bone in them may puncture the pouch, so avoid over-pulsing. Wrap the ends of the bones in parchment paper.
• When preparing game birds look out for pieces of shot and remove.
• Liquids such as stock or wine may be drawn out of the pouch when vacuum-sealing, so don't over-pulse. I often freeze them in ice cube trays and drop a cube or two into the pouch instead.
• Unless otherwise indicated the liquid in the pouch is discarded.
• Sear or brown game very quickly, as the game continues to cook. Because of this it's better to use a culinary blow torch to sear thin breasts of game birds, such as pheasant.
• Sous vide cooked game needs only a few minutes resting time, rather than the longer time required with conventional cooking.

Venison with Cranberries

Cranberries add a tartness to the dish, while orange and thyme add fragrance.

Serves: 2
Water bath cooking time: 6–8 hours

250g/9oz braising venison
2 tbsp oil
Freshly milled black pepper
To finish the dish
1 red onion
1 small sprig of thyme
1 small orange
Oil, for frying
300ml/½ pint well-flavoured game or chicken stock
¼ tsp ground allspice
1 small handful of cranberries, fresh or frozen
Salt and freshly milled black pepper

1 Fill the water bath and preheat to 60°C/140°F.
2 Cut the venison into bite-sized pieces and pat dry with kitchen paper.
3 Put the meat into two food pouches with some oil and a little pepper in each. Massage to mix the ingredients and push them into a single layer. Vacuum-seal.
4 When at temperature, put the pouches into the pouch rack and lower into the water bath, cover with the lid and cook for 6–8 hours.
5 To finish the dish, finely chop the onion. Pull the thyme leaves from the stalk and finely chop. Grate the zest from half the orange, cut in half and squeeze the juice from both halves.
6 Heat a little oil in a pan and cook the onion until softened and beginning to brown. Stir in the stock, thyme, allspice, cranberries, orange zest and juice, and a little salt and pepper. Bring just to the boil, reduce the heat and cook for 15–18 minutes, stirring occasionally. Season to taste.

7 Lift the pouches from the water bath. Remove the venison and dry on kitchen paper.
8 Heat a little oil in a heavy-based frying pan until very hot, add the venison and quickly sear until browned.
9 Stir the venison into the cranberry mix and serve.

At the end of step 4, the vacuum-sealed food pouches can be ice-chilled and refrigerated for up to four days, or frozen.

Venison with Vegetable Stir Fry

The timing for this recipe has to be just right. The meat has to be out and sliced as the stir-fried vegetables become ready.

Serves: 2
Water bath cooking time: 1–3 hours

2 venison loin steaks
2 tbsp oil
1 tsp freshly milled black pepper
To finish the dish
4 spring onions
175g/6oz selection of mini vegetables, such as carrots, courgettes,
    pak choi and leeks
Oil, for frying
150ml/¼ pint venison or chicken stock
2 tbsp light soy sauce
1 tbsp sweet chilli sauce
Salt and freshly milled black pepper

1   Fill the water bath and preheat to 60°C/140°F.
2   Pat the venison steaks dry with kitchen paper.
3   Put the steaks into two food pouches with the oil and pepper, then vacuum-seal.
4   When at temperature, put the pouches into the pouch holder and lower into the water bath, cover with the lid and cook for 1–3 hours.
5   To finish the dish, thinly slice the spring onions and mini vegetables.
6   Heat a little oil in a wok or large pan and cook all the vegetables for 4 minutes until they are starting to brown. Remove them from the pan with a slotted spoon. Stir in the stock, soy sauce, chilli sauce and seasoning. Bring just to the boil, then stir in the vegetables and cook for a few minutes until piping hot.

7   Lift the pouches from the water bath. Remove the steaks and pat dry with kitchen paper.

8   Heat a little oil in a heavy-based frying pan until very hot, add the venison and quickly sear until browned on all sides, or brush with a little oil and use a culinary blow torch.

9   Remove and drain the steaks and quickly cut into thin slices. Arrange the meat on a plate and serve with the vegetables.

At the end of step 4, the vacuum-sealed food pouches can be ice-chilled and refrigerated for up to four days, or frozen.

Venison Steaks with Whisky Mushrooms

Venison and whisky together make for a Scottish-themed dish.

Serves: 2
Water bath cooking time: 1–3 hours

2 x 175g/6oz venison loin steaks
2 tbsp oil
1 tsp freshly milled black pepper
To finish the dish
2 rashers smoked streaky bacon
200g/7oz mushrooms
1 eating apple
Oil, for frying
1 tsp lemon zest
150ml/¼ pint game or chicken stock
Salt and freshly milled black pepper
1 tbsp whisky

1   Fill the water bath and preheat to 60°C/140°F.
2   Pat the venison steaks dry with kitchen paper.
3   Put the steaks into two food pouches with the oil and pepper and vacuum-seal.
4   When at temperature, put the pouches into the pouch rack and lower into the water bath, cover with the lid and cook for 1-3 hours.
5   To finish the dish, finely chop the bacon and thinly slice the mushrooms. Core the apple and cut into wedges.
6   Heat a little oil in a pan and cook the bacon and mushrooms until browned. Add the lemon zest, stock and seasoning. Bring just to the boil, then cook for 10 minutes, adding the whisky at the end. Season to taste.

7   In another pan, heat a little oil and fry the apple slices until browned and cooked through. Lift the pouches from the water bath and remove the steaks. Pat dry with kitchen paper.

8   Heat a little oil in a heavy-based frying pan until very hot, add the venison and quickly sear until browned on all sides, or brush with a little oil and use a culinary blow torch.

9   Serve the venison with the bacon and mushroom mix, and the apple wedges on the side.

At the end of step 4, the vacuum-sealed food pouches can be ice-chilled and refrigerated for up to four days, or frozen.

Potted Game

Be sure to try this delicious treat – it's not just any old meat paste, and your sandwiches will never be the same again.

Serves: 6–8
Water bath cooking time: 4–8 hours

350g/12oz mix of pieces of boned game, such as pheasant, rabbit,
    grouse and venison
1 tbsp oil
2 tbsp chicken stock
Pinch of dried mixed herbs
Freshly milled black pepper
To finish the dish
3 juniper berries
1 tbsp vegetable oil
4 tbsp chicken stock
70g/2½oz unsalted butter
Pinch of ground mace
Salt and freshly milled black pepper
Hot toast, crusty bread, pickles and redcurrant jelly, to serve
For the clarified butter
60g/2¼oz unsalted butter (optional)

1   Fill the water bath and preheat to 60°C/140°F.
2   Trim the pieces of game, removing any skin and shot. Cut into bite-sized pieces and pat dry with kitchen paper.
3   Put the meat into a food pouch with the oil, stock, mixed herbs and a little pepper. Massage to mix the ingredients and push them into a single layer. Vacuum-seal.
4   When at temperature, put the pouch into the water bath, cover with the lid and cook for 4–8 hours.
5   To finish the dish, chop the juniper berries. Lift the pouch from the water bath. Remove the meat and dry on kitchen paper.
6   Heat the oil in a heavy-based frying pan until very hot, add the meat and quickly sear until browned all over.

7 With a slotted spoon, transfer the meat into a bowl. Add the stock, butter, juniper berries, ground mace and seasoning to the pan and heat until the butter has just melted. Scrape the contents of the pan onto the meat. Cool, chill for 15 minutes, then tip the meat mix into a food processor and blend. I like to leave some texture to the spread. Season to taste. Spoon into small ramekin dishes and smooth the tops. Cover with clingfilm and refrigerate.

8 If you like, clarified butter can be poured over the top of the spread to cover the surface. Heat the extra butter in a small pan until melted. Pour the clear yellow liquid into a jug, leaving the solids behind. Leave to cool a little, then pour into the ramekins to cover the meat.

9 Chill until ready to serve with hot toast, crusty bread, pickles and redcurrant jelly.

At the end of step 4, the vacuum-sealed food pouch can be ice-chilled and refrigerated for up to four days, or frozen.

Mixed Game with Chestnuts

Packs of diced game are available from many butchers, farmers' markets and supermarkets. They vary depending on the season and what's available, so the dish will taste slightly different each time it's made.

Serves: 4
Water bath cooking time: 4–8 hours

350g/12oz mix of pieces of boned game, such as pheasant, rabbit,
    grouse and venison
1 tbsp oil
Freshly milled black pepper
To finish the dish
1 onion
1 carrot
8 shelled, cooked chestnuts, canned, frozen or vacuum-packed
Oil, for frying
2 tsp Worcestershire sauce
300ml/½ pint game or chicken stock
2 tbsp balsamic vinegar
2 sprigs of thyme
Salt and freshly milled black pepper

1   Fill the water bath and preheat to 60°C/140°F.
2   Trim the pieces of game, removing any skin and shot. Cut into bite-sized pieces and pat dry with kitchen paper.
3   Put the meat into a food pouch with the oil and a little pepper. Massage to mix the ingredients and push them into a single layer. Vacuum-seal.
4   When at temperature, put the pouch into the water bath, cover with the lid and cook for 4–8 hours.
5   To finish the dish, finely chop the onion and carrot. Break the chestnuts into pieces.

6   Heat a little oil in a pan and cook the onion and carrot until softened and browned. Stir in the Worcestershire sauce, stock, balsamic vinegar, thyme sprigs and seasoning. Bring just to the boil and cook for 10 minutes. Stir in the chestnuts and cook for a further 10 minutes.

7   Lift the pouch from the water bath and remove the meat. Pat dry with kitchen paper and season.

8   Heat a little oil in a heavy-based frying pan until very hot, add the game pieces and quickly sear until browned on all sides. Stir the seared meat into the hot chestnut mix and serve immediately.

At the end of step 4, the vacuum-sealed food pouch can be ice-chilled and refrigerated for up to four days, or frozen.

Rabbit with Mustard Vegetables

Rabbit with mustard is a lovely, traditional way of bringing out the gaminess of the meat with the spiciness of the mustard.

Serves: 4
Water bath cooking time: 12–24 hours

500g/1lb 2oz boned rabbit
2 tbsp vegetable oil
2 tsp wholegrain mustard
Freshly milled black pepper
To finish the dish
1 onion
2 carrots
1 small leek
Oil, for frying
300ml/½ pint chicken stock
3 tbsp wholegrain mustard
1 bay leaf
Salt and freshly milled black pepper

1 Fill the water bath and preheat to 60°C/140°F.
2 Cut the rabbit into bite-sized pieces.
3 Heat a little oil in a pan until very hot. Add the rabbit and quickly sear the meat on all sides — you may need to do this in batches. Pat dry with kitchen paper and chill. (If not using immediately, remove and drain the meat, ice and refrigerate until cold.)
4 Put the meat into two food pouches and add some oil, mustard and a little pepper to each one. Massage the pouches to mix the meat and spices, push into a single, even layer and vacuum-seal.
5 When at temperature, put the pouches into the pouch rack and lower into the water bath, cover with the lid and cook for 12–24 hours.
6 To finish the dish, finely chop the onion and carrots. Thinly slice the leek.

7   Heat the oil in a large, heavy-based pan and fry the onion, carrots and leek until they begin to soften and brown. Stir in the stock, mustard, bay leaf and a little seasoning. Bring just to the boil, then cook for 20–30 minutes, stirring occasionally, until the vegetables are soft.

8   Lift the pouches from the water bath. Remove the meat and stir into the vegetable sauce in the pan. Season to taste and serve.

At the end of step 5, the vacuum-sealed food pouches can be ice-chilled and refrigerated for up to four days, or frozen.

Pheasant Breasts with Shallots and a Red Wine Sauce

For the best results, and to make sure the dish complements the wine, use a wine in your cooking that you like to drink.

Serves: 4
Water bath cooking time: 5–6 hours

4 pheasant breasts
4 tbsp oil
Freshly milled black pepper
To finish the dish
3 shallots
2 sprigs of thyme
Oil, for frying
300ml/½ pint game or chicken stock
150ml/¼ pint red wine
Salt and freshly milled black pepper
2 tbsp redcurrant jelly
Buttered shredded red cabbage, to serve

1   Fill the water bath and preheat to 60°C/140°F.
2   Pat the pheasant breasts dry with kitchen paper.
3   Put the meat into four food pouches and add the oil and a little pepper to each.
4   Press the air out of the pouches and vacuum-seal.
5   When at temperature, put the pouches into the pouch rack and lower into the water bath, cover with the lid and cook for 5–6 hours.
6   To finish the dish, finely chop the shallots. Pull the thyme leaves from the stalks and finely chop.
7   Heat some oil in a pan and cook the shallots until softened. Pour in the game or chicken stock and red wine, and add the thyme and seasoning. Bring to the boil, then turn the heat down and simmer until the sauce is reduced and beginning to thicken. Stir in the redcurrant jelly and season to taste.
8   Lift the pouches from the water bath and remove the pheasant breasts. Pat them dry with kitchen paper and season. Put them on a baking tray, brush with oil and brown the skin with a culinary blow torch or under a hot grill.
9   Serve immediately with the wine sauce and buttered red cabbage.

At the end of step 5, the vacuum-sealed food pouches can be ice-chilled and refrigerated for up to four days, or frozen.

8

Fruit

The fruity sous vide sensations in this chapter should prove irresistible. Desserts do well in the water bath, with all kinds of fruit retaining their vibrant colours, flavours and textures through the cooking process. These results apply equally well for hard and soft fruits, summer and winter fruits, and ready-to-eat dried fruits. Just contemplate the delights of Stuffed Apples with Cranberries and Apricots (see page 116), Spiced Plums with Pistachio Cream (see page 119) and a Mixed Fruit Compôte (see page 129). And there are recipes for mouth-watering pancakes, vanilla custard, a meringue pie and flavoured ice cream to complete the picture.

Stuffed Apples with Cranberries and Apricots

Always a family favourite. I've used eating apples, but this recipe is also delicious made with pears.

Serves: 4
Water bath cooking time: 1½ – 3 hours

4 large tart eating apples
1 tbsp lemon juice
4 ready-to-eat dried apricots
3 tbsp dried cranberries
2 tbsp melted butter
Good pinch of ground cinnamon
60g/2¼oz soft brown sugar
To finish the dish
Crème fraîche or ice cream, to serve

1   Fill the water bath and preheat to 84°C/183°F.
2   With an apple corer or a small sharp knife, remove the apple cores. Score a line round the middle of each apple to prevent them bursting, cutting just through the skin. Brush the lemon juice over the cut surfaces of the apples.
3   Roughly chop the apricots and cranberries, then tip them into a small bowl. Stir in the melted butter, cinnamon and sugar.
4   With a small spoon, push and press the fruity mixture into the cavity of each apple. Put each stuffed apple into individual pouches, keeping them upright, and vacuum-seal.
5   When at temperature, put the pouches into the water bath with the apples still upright. Put the rack horizontally on top of the apples to keep them submerged. Cover with the lid and cook for 1½–3 hours.
6   To finish the dish, lift the pouches from the water bath. Remove the apples from the pouches and place in individual bowls. Pour over the juices and serve with crème fraîche or ice cream.

At the end of step 5, the vacuum-sealed food pouches can be ice-chilled and refrigerated for up to four days.

Pears in Red Wine

Whole pears poached in red-wine syrup always make an elegant-looking dish.

Serves: 4
Water bath cooking time: 30 minutes–1 hour

250ml/9fl oz red wine or grape juice
5 tbsp caster sugar
4 pears
To finish the dish
Single cream, to pour

1   Pour the red wine or grape juice into a pan and stir in the sugar. Heat gently until the sugar has dissolved. Bring to the boil, then cook for 5–8 minutes until reduced by almost half. Leave to cool, then chill.
2   Fill the water bath and preheat to 84°C/183°F.
3   Leaving the stalks on, peel the pears. Remove and discard the core at the base. Put the pears into two food pouches, two in each. Pour the cold wine syrup over the pears and vacuum-seal.
4   When at temperature, put the pouches into the water bath. Put the rack horizontally on top of the pears to keep them submerged. Cover with the lid and cook for 30 minutes–1 hour.
5   To finish the dish, lift the pouches from the water bath. Leave the pears in the pouches for 40 minutes to cool.
6   Serve the pears with a little pouring cream.

At the end of step 4, the vacuum-sealed food pouches can be ice-chilled and refrigerated for up to four days.

Apricot Rice

A warming dessert that requires very little effort, as there's always a can of rice pudding to hand.

Serves: 4
Water bath cooking time: 30 minutes–1 hour

450g/1lb apricots
4 tbsp caster sugar
½ tsp vanilla extract
To finish the dish
400g can creamed rice

1   Fill the water bath and preheat to 84°C/183°F.
2   Halve the apricots and remove the stones.
3   Put the apricot halves into a food pouch. Add the sugar and vanilla extract. Shake the bag to mix the ingredients. Push the ingredients into a single, even layer and vacuum-seal.
4   When at temperature, put the pouch into the water bath, cover with the lid and cook for 30 minutes–1 hour.
5   To finish the dish, heat the creamed rice. Lift the pouch from the water bath. Spoon half of the apricots and the juices into a bowl and purée with a stick blender. Spoon the purée into serving bowls and top with the rice, and finally with the remaining apricot halves.

At the end of step 4, the vacuum-sealed food pouch can be ice-chilled and refrigerated for up to two days, or frozen.

Spiced Plums with Pistachio Cream

Cinnamon and star anise add an aromatic flavour to this dish, which also works well with greengages or apricots.

Serves: 4
Water bath cooking time: 30 minutes–1 hour

150ml/¼ pint red wine or orange juice
4 tbsp caster sugar
1 star anise
1 small cinnamon stick
600g/1lb 5oz plums
To finish the dish
200ml/7fl oz whipping cream
1–2 tbsp milk (optional)
90g/3¼oz toasted pistachio nuts
Small crisp biscuits, to serve

1   Pour the red wine or orange juice into a small pan and stir in the sugar, star anise and cinnamon stick. Heat gently until the sugar has dissolved. Bring to the boil and cook for 5 minutes. Leave to cool, then remove the star anise and cinnamon stick.
2   Fill the water bath and preheat to 84°C/183°F.
3   Halve the plums and remove the stones.
4   Put the plum halves into a food pouch in a single layer. Pour some of the spicy liquid over the fruit and vacuum-seal.
5   When at temperature, put the pouch into the water bath, cover with the lid and cook for 30 minutes–1 hour.
6   To finish the dish, lightly whip the cream. Finely chop the toasted pistachio nuts and stir into the whipped cream. If it is too thick, stir in a little milk.
7   Lift the pouch from the water bath. Spoon the hot plums into bowls, spoon over the spicy liquid and add a spoonful of pistachio cream along with one or two small biscuits.

At the end of step 5, the vacuum-sealed food pouch can be ice-chilled and refrigerated for up to four days, or frozen.

Raspberry and Cheese Toasts

A toasty treat. In place of the cream cheese you can use a mild soft goat's milk cheese instead.

Serves: 2
Water bath cooking time: 30 minutes–1 hour

225g/8oz raspberries
To finish the dish
2 thick slices brioche bread
3–4 tbsp cream cheese
2 tbsp maple syrup
A few toasted flaked almonds

1   Fill the water bath and preheat to 84°C/183°F.
2   Put the raspberries into a food pouch. Push them into a single, even layer and vacuum-seal.
3   When at temperature, put the pouch into the water bath, cover with the lid and cook for 30 minutes–1 hour.
4   To finish the dish, put the bread under a hot grill and toast on both sides. Spread cream cheese on top of each slice and grill until just starting to colour.
5   Lift the pouch from the water bath. Spoon the hot raspberries onto the hot bread. Drizzle a little maple syrup over the top and scatter over the almonds. Serve immediately.

At the end of step 3, the vacuum-sealed food pouch can be ice-chilled and refrigerated for up to four days, or frozen.

Cider Apples with Cardamom

Cardamom has a warm, spicy, sweet flavour that is lovely with apple, but does need to be used sparingly.

Serves: 4
Water bath cooking time: 45 minutes–2 hours

300ml/½ pint dry cider or unsweetened orange juice
4 tbsp caster sugar
Small pinch of ground cardamom
4 tart eating apples
1 tbsp lemon juice
To finish the dish
2 heaped tbsp butter
100g/3½oz granola-type cereal

1 Pour the cider or orange juice into a small pan and stir in the sugar and cardamom. Heat gently until the sugar has dissolved. Bring to the boil and cook for 5 minutes. Leave to cool.
2 Fill the water bath and preheat to 84°C/183°F.
3 Peel and core the apples and cut into 1cm/½in slices. Pour the lemon juice into a bowl with a little water. Dunk the apple slices in the lemon water and drain.
4 Put the apple slices into two food pouches in a single layer. Pour half of the cider syrup into each bag. Push the apples into a single, even layer and vacuum-seal.
5 When at temperature, put the pouches into the rack and lower into the water bath, cover with the lid and cook for 45 minutes–2 hours.
6 To finish the dish, heat the butter in a pan, add the cereal and cook until it is browned and piping hot.
7 Lift the pouches from the water bath. Spoon the hot apple slices into bowls. Pour over any cider syrup and scatter over the hot cereal topping.

At the end of step 5, the vacuum-sealed food pouches can be ice-chilled and refrigerated for up to four days.

Gooseberry and Elderflower Meringue Pie

Tart gooseberries scented with elderflower are the perfect combination with the crisp pastry case and soft meringue. Use individual pastry cases instead of one large one, if you prefer.

Serves: 4–6
Water bath cooking time: 30 minutes–1 hour

500g/1lb 2oz gooseberries
4 tbsp caster sugar
3 tbsp elderflower syrup
To finish the dish
20cm/8in cooked pastry flan case
3 egg whites
150g/5½oz golden caster sugar
1 tsp cornflour
1–2 tbsp icing sugar, sifted

1　Fill the water bath and preheat to 84°C/183°F.
2　Top and tail the gooseberries.
3　Put the gooseberries into a food pouch. Sprinkle over the sugar and pour over the elderflower syrup. Push the ingredients into a single, even layer and vacuum-seal
4　When at temperature, put the pouch into the water bath, cover with the lid and cook for 30 minutes–1 hour.
5　To finish the dish, preheat the oven to 190°C/175°C fan/gas 5.
6　Lift the pouch from the water bath and spoon the gooseberries into the flan case. Whisk the egg whites in a grease-free bowl until stiff peaks form. Whisk in half the sugar and, when stiff peaks form again, fold in the remaining sugar and the cornflour.
7　Swirl the meringue over the gooseberries and dust with the icing sugar. Bake for 15–20 minutes until golden. Serve hot or cold.

At the end of step 4, the vacuum-sealed food pouch can be ice-chilled and refrigerated for up to four days, or frozen.

Berries and Cherries

Deep colours and bursting with flavour, you can spoon the cooked fruit over slices of warm sponge cake or hot waffles.

Serves: 4–6
Water bath cooking time: 30 minutes–1 hour

250g/9oz mixed berries, such as blackberries, blueberries, loganberries
250g/9oz cherries
4 tbsp caster sugar
1 lemon
To finish the dish
Thick natural yogurt, to serve

1   Fill the water bath and preheat to 84°C/183°F.
2   Remove any stalks or leaves from the berries. Stone the cherries and cut in half.
3   Put the fruits into a food pouch, adding the sugar and lemon. Push the ingredients into a single, even layer and vacuum-seal.
4   When at temperature, put the pouch into the water bath, cover with the lid and cook for 30 minutes–1 hour.
5   To finish the dish, lift the pouches from the water bath. Spoon the hot fruits into bowls and top with a spoonful of thick yogurt.

At the end of step 4, the vacuum-sealed food pouch can be ice-chilled and refrigerated for up to four days, or frozen.

Peach and Meringue Trifle

My version of a trifle with peaches and cream, it's rather delicious.

Serves: 4–6
Water bath cooking time: 30 minutes–1 hour

4 peaches, not too soft
To finish the dish
200ml/7fl oz whipping cream, plus extra, to serve
Few drops of almond extract
2 meringue baskets or 6 small meringues
300ml/½ pint set lemon jelly

1   Fill the water bath and preheat to 84°C/183°F.
2   Halve the peaches and remove the stones.
3   Put the peach halves into a food pouch in single layer and vacuum-seal.
4   When at temperature, put the pouches into the water bath, cover with the lid and cook for 30 minutes–1 hour.
5   Lift the pouch from the water bath. Spoon the hot peaches onto a tray and leave to cool. Peel off the skins, then chill until cold.
6   To finish the dish, lightly whip the cream so that it still flows and add drops of almond extract to taste. Break the meringues into bite-sized pieces. With a fork, break the jelly into small pieces. Cut four of the peach halves into thin slices. Layer the peach slices, meringue, jelly and almond cream in tall glasses and top with a peach half. Pour over a little extra cream, if you like.

At the end of step 4, the vacuum-sealed food pouches can be ice-chilled and refrigerated for up to four days.

Rhubarb and Ginger Pancakes

For a guilty treat, serve these fruit pancakes warm with a scoop of good-quality vanilla ice cream.

Serves: 4
Water bath cooking time: 30 minutes–1 hour

450g/1lb rhubarb
150ml/¼ pint unsweetened apple juice
3 tbsp clear honey
To finish the dish
4 large sweet pancakes
60g/2¼oz crystallized ginger
150ml/¼ pint double cream
Icing sugar, to dust

1 Fill the water bath and preheat to 84°C/183°F.
2 Trim the rhubarb and cut into finger-length pieces. In a small bowl, mix together the apple juice and honey.
3 Put the rhubarb into two food pouches. Pour the apple juice and honey mixture into the pouches. Push the rhubarb into a single, even layer and vacuum-seal.
4 When at temperature, put the pouches into the rack and lower into the water bath, cover with the lid and cook for 30 minutes–1 hour.
5 To finish the dish, if serving warm, wrap the pancakes in foil and heat for a few minutes in a hot oven. Finely chop the crystallized ginger and stir into the cream.
6 Lift the pouches from the water bath and pour the juices into a small pan. Bring to the boil and cook until reduced to a thin syrup.
7 Spoon the hot rhubarb onto the pancakes and pour over the syrup. Fold the pancakes over the fillings, top with a spoonful of ginger cream and dust with icing sugar.

At the end of step 4, the vacuum-sealed food pouches can be ice-chilled and refrigerated for up to four days, or frozen.

Vanilla Custard

This traditional custard can be poured over desserts or used as the basis for ice creams or brûlées. Use a few drops of vanilla extract in place of the vanilla pod, if you prefer.

Makes about 300ml/½ pint
Serves: 4
Water bath cooking time: 15 minutes–1 hour

6 medium or large egg yolks
250ml/9fl oz whole milk
100g/3½oz caster sugar
1 vanilla pod

1   Fill the water bath and preheat to 82°C/181°F.
2   Put the egg yolks into a bowl and gently whisk or stir in the milk. When smooth, strain the mix into a jug and stir in the sugar. Cut the vanilla pod open along its length and use the back of a knife to scrape out the seeds into the egg and milk mixture.
3   Pour the mixture into a food pouch. Press the air out of the pouch with your hands, or stand the open pouch in a bowl of water so the air will be forced out. Seal the pouch. Do not vacuum-seal.
4   When at temperature, put the pouch into the water bath, cover with the lid and cook for 15 minutes–1 hour. During this time, lift the pouch out of the water bath every 3–5 minutes, massage the pouch to mix the ingredients together, then return it to the water and continue cooking.
5   Lift the pouch from the water bath and serve the custard hot or ice-chilled.

At the end of step 4, the vacuum-sealed food pouch can be ice-chilled and refrigerated for up to three days.

Berry and Cherry Ice Cream

This ice cream is made using two of the sous vide recipes in this chapter, the vanilla custard and the berries and cherries.

Serves: 4–6

300ml/½ pint double cream
1 quantity Vanilla Custard (see page 126)
150ml/¼ pint thick natural yogurt
Clear honey, to taste
1 quantity Berries and Cherries (see page 123), drained and chilled
Wafer biscuits, to serve

1   Pour the cream into a bowl and lightly whisk until it forms soft peaks.
2   In a separate bowl, mix together the custard, yogurt and honey, to taste. Carefully fold in the whipped cream. Swirl the drained mixed berries through the mixture.
3   Spoon the ice cream mixture into a freezer container, level the surface, and freeze for about 30 minutes until the ice cream begins to ice around the edges. Stir the mixture, cover again and return to the freezer for another 30 minutes. Repeat the process once, then leave to freeze. Alternatively, churn in an ice cream maker.
4   Put the ice cream in the fridge for 15 minutes before serving to soften a little. Scoop into bowls and serve with wafer biscuits.

Chocolate and Raspberry Nutty Ice Cream

So moreish it won't last long in the freezer. This also uses other sous vide recipes from this chapter.

Serves: 4–6

125g/4½oz good-quality dark chocolate
150ml//¼ pint double cream
Icing sugar, to taste
1 quantity Vanilla Custard (see page 126)
300ml/½ pint thick natural yogurt, drained
3 tbsp chopped toasted hazelnuts
Extra grated chocolate and toasted nuts, to serve
1 quantity raspberries from Raspberry and Cheese Toasts (see page 120), chilled
Wafer biscuits, to serve

1   Coarsely grate the chocolate. Pour the cream into a bowl and lightly whisk until it forms soft peaks. Sweeten with a little icing sugar to taste.
2   In a separate bowl, mix together the custard, yogurt, chopped hazelnuts and grated chocolate. Carefully fold in the whipped cream and swirl the raspberries through the mixture.
3   Spoon the ice cream mixture into a freezer container, level the surface, and freeze for 30 minutes until the ice cream begins to ice around the edges. Stir the mixture, cover again and return to the freezer for another 30 minutes. Repeat the process once, then leave to freeze. Alternatively, churn in an ice cream maker.
4   Put the ice cream in the fridge for 15 minutes before serving to soften a little. Scoop the ice cream into bowls, sprinkle over extra chopped nuts and grated chocolate, and add a wafer biscuit.

Mixed Fruit Compôte

Compôte is usually served cold but I like to serve it hot as well. Fresh and dried fruits become juicy and succulent when cooked together with a little spice and apple juice. Spoon this hot or cold over porridge, spread onto waffles or simply serve with a spoonful of crème fraîche.

Serves: 4
Water bath cooking time: 1–2 hours

1 eating apple
175g/6oz mixed dried ready-to-eat fruits, such as prunes,
   blueberries, figs, apricots, pears
60g/2¾oz sultanas
2 tsp lemon zest
Good pinch of ground cinnamon
2 tbsp light brown sugar
150ml/¼ pint unsweetened apple juice
To finish the dish
Thick natural yogurt, to serve

1   Fill the water bath and preheat to 84°C/183°F.
2   Core the apple, leaving the skin on, and roughly chop. If necessary, cut any large pieces of the dried fruits into bite-sized pieces. Put the chopped apple, dried fruits and sultanas into a bowl. Stir in the lemon zest, cinnamon, sugar and apple juice.
3   Spoon the fruit mixture into two food pouches, making sure you don't overfill them. Push the ingredients into a single, even layer and vacuum-seal.
4   When at temperature, put the pouches into the rack and lower into the water bath. Cover with the lid and cook for 1–2 hours.
5   To finish the dish, lift the pouches from the water bath. Serve the compôte hot or leave to cool and chill, then serve cold with a spoonful of yogurt.

At the end of step 4, the vacuum-sealed food pouch can be ice-chilled and refrigerated for up to four days or frozen

9
Hot Pepper Sauce

9
Useful Extras

You've done a splendid job cooking to perfection your vegetables, meat or fish using your trusty sous vide. All you want now is one of those little extras – the sauces, toppings, salsas or dressings – to add a mouth-watering flavour combination and a touch of pizzazz to your completed meal.

You'll find here a useful selection of recipes and quick tips for hot and cold, savoury and sweet accompaniments, tailor-made for that final flourish. There are also some great ideas for storable items, such as the flavoured oils and vinegars used as dressings – keep any leftovers in a jar in the fridge – and the flavoured butters, which should also be stored in the fridge or in the freezer before being used.

Salsas and the toppings with nuts, seeds or breadcrumbs are best made fresh for serving, while the hot sauces show once again how adaptable your sous vide machine can be.

Hot Pepper Sauce

Swirl into soups or stir-fries for colour and spice.

Serves: 4
Water bath cooking time: 45 minutes–1½ hours

4 red peppers
1 red chilli
Pinch of dried thyme
2 tbsp vegetable stock
1 tbsp olive oil
Salt and freshly milled black pepper

1   Fill the water bath and preheat to 84°C/183°F.
2   Cut the peppers and chilli in half, remove and discard the seeds and stalks, then chop finely.
3   Put the chopped peppers and chilli into a food pouch. Add the thyme, stock, oil and a little seasoning. Push the ingredients into a shallow layer and vacuum-seal.
4   When at temperature, put the pouches into the water bath, cover with the lid and cook for 45 minutes–1½ hours.
5   To finish the dish, lift the pouch from the water bath, pour the juices from the bag into a pan and heat until reduced by half. Pour the contents of the pouch into the pan with the juices. Use a stick blender to whizz the pepper mixture until smooth. Heat and season to taste.

At the end of step 4, the vacuum-sealed food pouch can be ice-chilled and refrigerated for up to three days, or frozen.

Tomato Sauce

For best results, use tomatoes that are full of flavour. Spread over pizza bases or stir into piping hot pasta or noodles.

Serves: 4
Water bath cooking time: 1–2½ hours

450g/1lb tomatoes
1 sun-dried tomato
1 small red onion
1 garlic clove
1 tbsp olive oil
2 tbsp vegetable stock
¼ tsp ground oregano
Pinch of sugar
Salt and freshly milled black pepper
To finish the dish
8 stoned black olives
1 small handful of basil leaves

1   Fill the water bath and preheat to 84°C/183°F.
2   To skin the tomatoes, pierce their skins and put them into a bowl of piping hot water for 30–40 seconds until the skins wrinkle. Lift the tomatoes from the bowl and peel off the skins. Cut in half and remove the cores and seeds. Roughly chop the tomatoes and the sun-dried tomato. Finely chop the onion and clove.
3   Put the chopped tomatoes, onion and garlic into a food pouch. Add the oil, stock, oregano, sugar and a little seasoning. Push the ingredients into a single, even layer and vacuum-seal.
4   When at temperature, put the pouch into the water bath, cover with the lid and cook for 1–2½ hours.
5   To finish the dish, lift the pouch from the water bath, pour the juices from the bag into a pan and heat until reduced by half. Pour the contents of the pouch into the pan with the juices. Use a stick blender to whizz the tomato mixture until smooth. Heat, stir in the olives and basil and season to taste.

At the end of step 4, the vacuum-sealed food pouch can be ice-chilled and refrigerated for up to four days, or frozen.

Tomato and Chilli Salsa

Salsa is the Spanish name for a sauce made with raw ingredients. Always alive and refreshing, serve a spoonful on the side to add colour and zing. Use just one chilli if you prefer less 'heat'.

Serves: 4–6

1 red onion
1 garlic clove
2–3 red chillies
4–6 ripe tomatoes
1 small bunch of basil
1 lime
3–4 tbsp olive or sunflower oil
Pinch of sugar
Salt and freshly milled black pepper

1   Finely chop the onion and crush the garlic clove. Cut the chillies in half, remove and discard the seeds and stalks, and finely chop. Slice the tomatoes in half, remove the cores and roughly chop. Pull the leaves from the basil and finely snip.
2   Zest the lime, cut in half and squeeze the juices into a bowl.
3   Add the olive or sunflower oil, sugar and lime zest to the juice. Mix in the prepared onion, garlic, chillies, tomatoes and basil. Season to taste.
4   Cover and chill for an hour for the flavours to develop.

Red Pepper Salsa

A bright and peppery salsa that's great with grilled dishes.

Serves: 4–6

2 red peppers
3–4 tbsp olive or sunflower oil
1 red onion
1 bunch of watercress
1 unwaxed lemon
Salt and freshly milled black pepper

1　Brush the skin of the red peppers with a little of the oil. Cook under a hot grill until the skins are blackened, turning frequently. Put the charred peppers into a freezer bag and leave to cool.
2　Peel the skins from the peppers, remove the stalks, cut in half and scrape out the seeds. Cut into thin strips or roughly chop. Finely chop the onion. Pull the watercress leaves from the stalks. Leave the small leaves whole and tear any large ones in half.
3　Zest the lemon, cut in half and squeeze the juices into a bowl.
4　Add the olive or sunflower oil and lemon zest to the juice. Mix in the prepared onion, red peppers and watercress. Season to taste.
5　Cover and chill for an hour for the flavours to develop.

Mango and Cucumber Salsa

Light, colourful and refreshing, serve with with Shredded Beef Tortillas (see page 54), Fish Cakes (see page 36) or Chicken Fritters (see page 91).

Serves: 4

1 large mango
1 small cucumber
1 red chilli
1 small bunch of coriander
1 orange
3–4 tbsp olive or sunflower oil
Salt and freshly milled black pepper

1   Peel the mango and cut the flesh away from the stone or pit. Cut the flesh into small pieces. Peel the cucumber, cut in half lengthways and scoop out the seeds. Cut the cucumber into thin slices. Cut the chilli in half, remove and discard the seeds and stalk, then finely chop. Pull the leaves from the coriander and then chop.
2   Zest half the orange, cut it in half and squeeze the juices into a bowl.
3   Add the olive or sunflower oil and orange zest to the juice. Mix in the prepared mango, cucumber, chilli and coriander. Season to taste.
4   Cover and chill for an hour for the flavours to develop.

Walnut and Toasted Sesame Seed Dressing

Drizzle over crisp salad leaves such as rocket, baby spinach, mizuna and lamb's lettuce. I sometimes add a chopped apple and a few seedless grapes that have been halved. Or serve as a dip with sticks of carrots, pepper and celery.

Serves: 2–4

1 garlic clove
1 small bunch of parsley
6–8 walnut halves
3 tbsp toasted sesame seeds
150ml/¼ pint Greek yogurt
1 tsp clear honey
Salt and freshly milled black pepper
A little water or milk (optional)

1 Crush the garlic clove. Finely chop the parsley and walnuts. Using a mortar and pestle or a food processor, crush the sesame seeds.
2 Spoon the yogurt into a bowl and stir in the honey.
3 Mix in the prepared ingredients and season to taste with salt and pepper. If the dressing seems too thick, thin with a little cold water or milk.
4 Cover and chill for an hour for the flavours to develop.

Chive and Fennel Dressing

This is perfect with cooked fish and shellfish dishes. If you have a clean jam-jar to hand, put all the ingredients into the jar and give it a good shake to mix.

Serves: 2–4

1 small bunch of fennel leaves
1 small bunch of chives
½ small lime
6 tbsp olive oil
2 tsp cider vinegar
Pinch of paprika
Salt and freshly milled black pepper

1   Finely chop the fennel leaves and snip the chives with scissors. Grate the lime peel to give about 1 tbsp of zest, then squeeze out the juice.
2   Pour the lime juice and zest, olive oil and cider vinegar into a small bowl and whisk together. Stir in the fennel and chives, then season to taste with paprika, salt and black pepper.
3   Cover and chill for an hour for the flavours to develop.

Gremolata

Traditionally this bright, fresh garnish is sprinkled over Osso Buco, the Italian veal dish, but I like to use it with most savoury dishes. For the best flavour, prepare on the day.

Serves: 4

1 large bunch of flat-leaf parsley
2 large fat garlic cloves
1 unwaxed lemon

1   Pull the leaves from the parsley stalks and finely chop. Crush and finely chop the garlic cloves. Finely grate or zest the lemon.
2   Mix the three ingredients together in a bowl, cover and chill.

Pesto

An Italian uncooked sauce to stir into pasta. Traditionalists would frown, but I often blitz the ingredients in my food processor rather than using a mortar and pestle.

Serves: 4–6

1 garlic clove
1 large bunch of basil
1 handful of toasted pine nuts
3–4 tbsp freshly grated Pecorino or Parmesan cheese
200ml/7fl oz olive oil plus extra, if needed
Ground sea salt, to taste

1   Chop the garlic clove. Pull the basil leaves from the stalks.
2   Put the garlic, basil leaves and pine nuts into a food processor and blitz until finely chopped.
3   Mix in the Pecorino or Parmesan cheese. Add the oil in two batches and mix to make a soft consistency, adding more oil if necessary. Season to taste with a little sea salt.
4   Cover and chill until needed. Keep the pesto in the fridge, but make sure there is a layer of oil on the surface and it should keep for two weeks.

Roasted Nuts and Seeds

I always have a jar or two of seeds in the cupboard. They make an instant topping, just scattered very lightly over cooked or fresh foods or stirred into salads, or made into a crunchy topping on cooked fish fillets. Use your favourite seeds and nuts.

Serves: 6–8

280g/10oz shelled unsalted nuts, such as pecans, hazelnuts, almonds or peanuts
2 tbsp sunflower oil
1 tbsp cider vinegar
1 tbsp soft brown sugar
2 tsp paprika
1 tbsp njgella seeds
100g/3½oz sesame seeds
125g/4½oz sunflower seeds

1 Preheat the oven to 190°C/175°C fan /gas 5.
2 Roughly chop the nuts.
3 In a bowl, mix together the oil, vinegar, brown sugar and paprika. Add the nuts and seeds, then mix until they are well coated. Spread thinly over baking sheets.
4 Put into the hot oven and cook for 10 minutes until lightly toasted.
5 Leave until cold, then store in a screw-topped jar or an airtight container.

Crunchy Crumbs

A useful topping to scatter over vegetables, fish or meat. Use day-old bread, as it will
be drier and makes a better crumb.

Serves: 4

4 slices day-old sourdough bread
2 large garlic cloves (optional)
1 large unwaxed lemon or lime
Sunflower oil, for frying
Ground white pepper, to taste

1   Cut the crusts from the bread slices and use a food processor to
    make coarse breadcrumbs.
2   Crush the garlic, if using, and finely grate the lemon or lime.
3   Heat a little oil and, when hot, add the garlic, if using, and the
    breadcrumbs. Cook, stirring all the time, until the crumbs are
    lightly browned.
4   Remove the pan from the heat and quickly stir in the grated
    lemon or lime rind, seasoning with pepper to taste. Use immediately.

Flavoured Oils

Using the sous vide is a very exciting and fast method of 'pushing' flavours into both oils and vinegars. It's fun to experiment with your favourite flavour combinations. Drizzle or splash over salads and raw or cooked dishes; alternatively use as the basis for marinades, dips and salad dressings.

Makes approximately 200ml/7fl oz
Water bath cooking time: at least 30 minutes

For each flavour:
200ml/7fl oz oil, such as olive, vegetable, rapeseed or sunflower

Plus choose one of the following options:
For Walnut and Lime
Peel of 1 lime and a small handful of broken walnut pieces
For Orange
Peel of 1 large orange
For Lemon and Parsley
Peel of a lemon and a handful of parsley sprigs
For Mustard and Chilli
2 tbsp wholegrain mustard and 1 halved red chill

1   Fill the water bath and preheat to 84°C/183°F.
2   For the Walnut and Lime, Orange, or Lemon and Parsley options, blanch the citrus peel in boiling water for 60 seconds. Refresh in cold water and dry on kitchen paper.
3   For the Mustard and Chilli option, blanch the chilli in boiling water for 30 seconds. Refresh in cold water and dry on kitchen paper.
4   For all options, pour the oil into a food pouch and add your chosen flavouring. Press the air out of the pouch with your hands or stand the open pouch in a bowl of water so the air will be forced out. Seal the pouch. Do not vacuum-seal.
5   When at temperature, put the pouch into the water bath, cover with the lid and cook for 30 minutes.
6   Lift the pouch from the machine. Massage the pouch to mix the ingredients, then leave to cool.
7   Pour the contents of the pouch through a fine-meshed sieve into a sterilized screw-topped bottle and store in the fridge.

Flavoured Vinegars

Use flavoured vinegars in dressings, marinades and light, quick pickle mixes.

Makes approximately 200ml/7fl oz
Water bath cooking time: at least 30 minutes

For each flavour
200ml/7fl oz vinegar, such as red wine, cider or white wine

Plus choose one of the following options:
For Mustard and Chive
1 small bunch of finely chopped chives and 2 tbsp mustard seeds, crushed
For Raspberry
1 small handful of raspberries, thawed if frozen, and 2 tsp sugar
For Garlic and Lemon
3 garlic cloves, peeled and halved, and the zest of ½ lemon
For Lemongrass and Rosemary
1 thumb-sized piece of lemongrass, roughly chopped, and the leaves of
   2 rosemary stalks

1   Fill the water bath and preheat to 84°C/183°F.
2   For the Mustard and Chive option, blanch the chives in boiling water for 30 seconds. Refresh in cold water and dry on kitchen paper.
3   For the Garlic and Lemon option, blanch the garlic and lemon in boiling water for 60 seconds. Refresh in cold water and dry on kitchen paper.
4   For the Lemongrass and Rosemary option, blanch the lemongrass and rosemary in boiling water for 60 seconds. Refresh in cold water and dry on kitchen paper.

5   For all options, pour the vinegar into a food pouch and add your chosen flavouring. Press the air out of the pouch with your hands or stand the open pouch in a bowl of water so the air will be forced out. Seal the pouch. Do not vacuum-seal.

6   When at temperature, put the pouch into the water bath, cover with the lid and cook for 30 minutes.

7   Lift the pouch from the machine. Massage the pouch to mix the ingredients and leave to cool.

8   Pour the contents of the pouch through a fine-meshed sieve into a sterilized screw-topped bottle and store in the fridge.

Flavoured Butters

A fridge or freezer essential. To make, these savoury and sweet butters give a quick burst of flavour to your cooking. Add a flavoured butter pat into the cooking pouch when cooking vegetables, fish, meat and fruits. Alternatively, stir into hot rice or pasta, or melt on pancakes or waffles.

Serves: 6–8

For each flavour:
150g/5½oz salted or unsalted butter, softened

Plus choose one of the following savoury options:
For Wholegrain Mustard and Chives
2 tbsp wholegrain mustard and a few chive stalks, finely snipped
For Lemon, Garlic and Oregano
3 tsp lemon zest, 1 garlic clove, crushed, and a few oregano leaves, finely chopped
For Blue Cheese
60g/2¼oz Dolcelatte or Blue Stilton cheese
For Black Olives, Pine Nuts, Lime and Parsley
4 black olives, finely chopped, a few toasted pine nuts, chopped, 1 tsp lime zest, and a few sprigs of parsley, finely chopped
For Fennel and Lemon
2 tsp toasted ground fennel seeds and 2 tsp lime juice
For Parmesan, Spring Onion and Celery
1 tbsp grated Parmesan cheese, half a spring onion, finely chopped, and a few celery leaves, finely chopped

Plus for each savoury option, add
Salt and freshly milled black pepper, to taste

Or choose one of the following sweet options:
For Orange and Rum
2 tsp orange zest, 1 tbsp orange juice and 1 tbsp rum or grape juice
For Hazelnut and Lime
3 tbsp chopped toasted hazelnuts and 1 tsp lime zest
For Ginger
1 tbsp crystallised ginger, finely chopped
For Lavender and Orange
4 lavender leaves, finely chopped, and 1 tsp orange zest

Plus for each sweet option, add
Icing sugar, to taste

1   Put the softened butter into a bowl.
2   Stir in your selection of ingredients and season or sweeten to taste.
3   Cover the bowl and chill for 30 minutes. Put the flavoured butter onto a sheet of baking parchment or clingfilm and roll it into a sausage shape, then wrap in clingfilm and chill until needed.
4   Cut into slices as required.

The flavoured butter slices can be frozen. Layer between sheets of baking parchment in a lidded freezer container.

Hazelnut Caramel Sauce

This is probably the easiest way of transforming condensed milk into caramel. I welcome it after having spent years stirring the milk in a pan on the hob, trying so hard not to let it burn. I've added a few nuts and sea salt for an up-to-the-mark taste, which is so fashionable. A little lemon juice adds a sharpness, or just use au naturel.

Serves: 4–6
Water bath cooking time: 45 minutes–2 hours

397g can condensed milk
To finish the dish
1 small handful of toasted finely chopped hazelnuts
Pinch of finely ground sea salt
Lemon juice

1   Fill the water bath and preheat to 84°C/183°F.
2   Pour the condensed milk into a food pouch. Gently press the air out of the bag and seal. Do not vacuum-seal.
3   When at temperature, put the pouch into the water bath, cover with the lid and cook for 45 minutes–2 hours.
4   To finish the sauce, open the pouch, add the chopped nuts and a little salt and lemon juice, to taste. Massage the pouch to mix the ingredients together.

At the end of step 3, the vacuum-sealed food pouch can be ice-chilled and refrigerated for seven days. Reheat the pouch in the water bath to soften the caramel.

Chocolate Sauce

Chocolate is always a favourite – with adults and children alike. Pour the sauce over fruit, ice cream, pancakes and waffles.

Serves: 4
Water bath cooking time: 15–30 minutes

225g/8oz good-quality dark chocolate
250ml/9fl oz double cream
1 tbsp golden syrup

1   Fill the water bath and preheat to 60°C/140°F.
2   Break the chocolate into pieces and drop into a food pouch. Pour in the cream and golden syrup. Gently press the air out of the bag and seal. Do not vacuum-seal.
3   When at temperature, put the pouch into the water bath, cover with the lid and cook for 15–30 minutes until the chocolate has melted.
4   Massage the pouch to mix the ingredients together.

At the end of step 3, the vacuum-sealed food pouch can be ice-chilled and refrigerated for seven days. Reheat the pouch in the water bath to soften the sauce.

Plum Sauce with Red Wine

A bright and colourful sauce that goes well with most desserts. It is equally good when flavoured with a little ground rosemary or cardamom in place of the cinnamon.

Serves: 4
Water bath cooking time: 45 minutes–1½ hours

450g/1lb ripe plums
4 tbsp light brown sugar
Pinch of ground cinnamon
To finish the dish
150ml/¼ pint red wine or red grape juice

1   Fill the water bath and preheat to 84°C/183°F.
2   Halve the plums and remove the stones. Roughly chop the fruit.
3   Put the chopped plums into a food pouch. Add the sugar and cinnamon and shake the bag to mix the ingredients. Push the ingredients into a single, even layer and vacuum-seal.
4   When at temperature, put the pouch into the water bath, cover with the lid and cook for 45 minutes–1½ hours.
5   To finish the dish, pour the wine or grape juice into a pan, bring to the boil, then simmer until reduced by half.
6   Lift the pouch from the water bath and pour the contents into the pan with the wine. Use a stick blender to whizz the plum mixture until smooth. Serve hot or cold.

At the end of step 4, the vacuum-sealed food pouch can be ice-chilled and refrigerated for up to four days, or frozen.

Index